WHAT IT TAKES

MARK BOURIS is the Executive Chairman of Yellow Brick Road Wealth Management and has over 25 years experience in the finance and property sectors. He currently holds Executive and Non-Executive Chairmanships with technology company TZ Limited, healthcare company Anteo Diagnostics Limited, and resource company Serena Resources Limited.

Mark is Adjunct Professor for Banking & Finance and Business Law & Tax at the University of New South Wales Australian School of Business and he sits on the UNSW Australian School of Business Advisory Council Board. He is also a member of Deputy Prime Minister Wayne Swan's Financial Sector Advisory Council, and a board member of the Sydney Roosters.

Mark holds a Bachelor of Commerce and a Masters of Commerce from the University of New South Wales, as well as an Honorary Doctorate of Business from the University of New South Wales and an Honorary Doctorate of Letters from the University of Western Sydney.

He is also the host of *The Celebrity Apprentice Australia*.

WHAT IT TAKES

AN ATTITUE OF HARD WORK, COMMITMENT AND PURPOSE

MARK BOURIS

ALLEN&UNWIN
SYDNEY • MELBOURNE • AUCKLAND • LONDON

Every effort has been made to provide accurate and authoritative information in this book. Neither the publisher nor the author accepts any liability for injury, loss or damage caused to any person acting as a result of information in this book nor for any errors or omissions. Readers are advised to obtain advice from a licensed financial planner before acting on the information contained in this book.

First published in 2013

Arena Books, an imprint of
Allen & Unwin
83 Alexander Street
Crows Nest NSW 2065
Australia
Phone: (61 2) 8425 0100
Email: info@allenandunwin.com
Web: www.allenandunwin.com

Cataloguing-in-Publication details are available
from the National Library of Australia
www.trove.nla.gov.au

ISBN 978 1 74175 685 2

Printed and bound in Australia by Pegasus Media & Logistics

30 29 28 27 26

MIX
Paper from
responsible sources
FSC
www.fsc.org
FSC® C008194

The paper in this book is FSC® certified.
FSC® promotes environmentally responsible,
socially beneficial and economically viable
management of the world's forests.

To my sons. Each of you has taken your own path and I'm very proud of who you have become. Keep at it.

To Mark Abernethy, who helped me write this book. Thank you.

CONTENTS

Introduction ix

1   Success is attitude 1

2   Putting in the hard work 9

3   Being relentless 19

4   Know your purpose 28

5   What it takes 38

6   So you want your own business 54

7   The reality of business ownership 63

8   What sort of business owner are you? 74

9   Business types 84

10 Employees 102

11 Growth-focused employees 109

12 Building a business 120

13 Getting started—the business plan 132

14 Running a business 147

15 Building your team 158

16 Leadership 172

17 Towards an exit 187

18 Getting out 199

19 Your business and *you* 212

20 Stepping away from yourself 223

21 Looking after yourself 232

INTRODUCTION

Don't read this if you want the secret to success. There is no secret. There are no laws of attraction, no shortcuts, no tricks of the trade. People who succeed in business, careers and in life do so because they work at it.

There are many people who will tell you about their secret of success. I'm not one of them. I don't think about 'success' in the way many people do because I see it as personal achievement measured against what it is you set out to do.

I don't think in terms of secrets. I think in terms of what it takes. I think about how you get to where you want to go, how to change what you need to change and how to identify what that might be.

When I think about what it takes to be successful, I start from those things you can absolutely control—attitude, self-reflection, skills—and then I push further out into the aspects that you can influence—strategy, team-building, advice—and, finally, I think about the great unknowns of business and life, and what you have to have done in preparation for them. Which takes us back to the start.

So, my own approach to what some people call success is really to start with myself because that's where I can exert the most control. And as I get further into the complexity, risk and chaos of the economy and the market, I lose some control, which is why I want to ensure I have started with the basics.

I make this distinction early in order to distinguish between those things you can change and those things you can't. It isn't just that you save time and energy by understanding this, but you also divert more of your resources towards the aspects where your own efforts can control the outcome. For instance, because of my profile and the fact that I am seen as a business builder, I attract many people who want to show me their ideas, have me as an investor, ask me to mentor them or just want advice about whether it's a good time to buy property.

And I've noticed that many of the questions are of the 'huge' variety. People read the papers and see the news about what's happened to the iron ore price or what happened to Telstra's share price or what the Reserve Bank of Australia (RBA) did with interest rates. They obsess about when the global financial crisis (GFC) will be over or what's happening to sovereign debt. It becomes like an addiction to hear this overwhelming news, and the waves of numbers and indices create confusion and panic.

Me? I say forget about huge—keep it simple. Sweat the small stuff. Don't be overwhelmed, be focused. Listen less to what the Organisation for Economic Co-operation and Development

(OECD) says and more to what your customers, your staff or your clients are saying.

To those people who worry about European debt or gross domestic product (GDP) growth, I say: ignore it. Unless your business model specifically requires reference to these massive concepts, they are beyond you. And I'll give you another tip: they're beyond Marius Kloppers and James Packer and Glenn Stevens, too. It's just that these people have to know what the numbers mean because they're deciding whether to spend a billion dollars on a coalmine or to raise interest rates, or where to build a new casino.

You see, no one is bigger than the cycle. The cycle of business affects everyone and yet no one person can influence it. Usually, the cycle is a long, flat series of ups and downs. We see it in house prices, inflation, retail sales, wage inflation. There are large and small businesses that can build a business case or a new product based on these long cycles: for instance, a bank might introduce a low doc loan for the boom real estate times. A small mortgage broker might specialise in low doc lending to take advantage of this. A corporation might hire and fire on these long cycles, but smart employees learn to read the signs and retrain in something more useful or go back to university, or skip to another employer who wants the skills they have.

But then there are times when the cycle shortens up and deepens. It no longer looks like undulating curves: it's vertical lines going up and down like a seismograph. In these times—which the GFC has initiated—not even big corporations, banks or sometimes even governments can influence or plan properly for the cycle. It is bigger than everyone: just ask General Motors or the Greek government.

So where does that leave you?

It leaves you in the position of having to control what you can control, change what you can change, and influence what you can influence. You start with yourself; move onto your partners, employees and team members; and then further out into the market and the economy.

•

There are 2.7 million business owners in Australia. They run enterprises that range from sole practitioners to large family-owned businesses that employ thousands of people. Given that we have a labour participation rate of 12 million, you can see that Australians are a fairly enterprising bunch. Almost one in four of those gainfully employed are business owners. Yet they pay 60 per cent of private enterprise wages and contribute 30 per cent of GDP.

This is a huge contribution and it's typical of Australia and Australians that we downplay this entrepreneurship in favour of talking too much about public companies and government budgets. We punch above our weight, which is something we acknowledge in sport, entertainment and the sciences but not in our business activity. In reality, we're a hard-working, enterprising nation filled with people who will not be beaten.

I think this can be attributed to our beginnings in which people travelled from one end of the world to the other, and carved out whatever they could with hard work, sacrifice and risk. The convicts didn't have a choice: once they were freed, what else was there to do but ply a trade and work their backs off? The people with a bit of capital didn't have it any easier. They could buy land out west, but all they were really buying was decades of backbreaking toil, drought, floods, land-clearing and bushfires.

The waves of immigration followed the English, Irish, Scottish and Welsh: Chinese, Italian, German, Greek, Lebanese, Vietnamese, Cambodian, Indian, Sir Lankan, Iraqi, Afghani. Each wave of migration brought with it the most enterprising and adventurous DNA. It brought people restless for change and desperate to leave the conditions which held back themselves and their families. Australia has its own little class system, and so each wave of migration—the convicts, the Irish, the Chinese, the Lebanese, the Vietnamese—found themselves outside the social elites and therefore had to forge their own success stories. And if you stand outside the dominant social order, your most available avenue is to create a business that fills a basic human need: food, shelter, etc. So it's no accident that you find the 'outsiders' of Australian history building the pubs, opening the restaurants, pouring the concrete, tiling the roofs and growing the crops.

My own family followed these classic patterns. On my mother's side, her people—the Collits—built an inn circa 1823 on the road that the explorers and early settlers forged through the Blue Mountains west of Sydney. The patriarch was a freed convict and also Irish, so there was no easy entry into colonial society. But there was a new road, the Great Western Highway, going to the new agricultural centres out west, and that meant travellers who needed a meal, a drink and a bed to sleep in. They built the Collits Inn on a site in the Blue Mountains, and there's still a hotel on that original site, by the way, suggesting that it was as good an idea now as it was back then.

The immigrants to this country all came from cultures where business had been a way of life for thousands of years. In Asia and the Middle East, the grinding work ethic of starting a business and working yourself to a standstill was an accepted part of life. When the immigrants came from these parts of the world, they brought that business DNA, but they could apply it freely in a rich, open country where there was wealth, land, time and social mobility. And because of the conditions in this country, the immigrants' work practices flourished. It was like taking a formula that works well enough in a place where the resources are exhausted, but when it lands in the abundant fields of Australia, it becomes turbocharged.

The waves of people who filled up this country, but had no social standing, had to do something that has become a catchcry of Australia: they were urged to *back yourself*. I love this saying because it has two meanings: one is the sense of laying a bet, and backing yourself in a race; the other sense is financial—that if you can't find a bank or investor to back you, you'll have to invest in yourself.

I believe that Australia's unspoken culture—the one that isn't about beer, beaches and sport—is its culture of backing yourself. It doesn't mean that every person who starts a small business is going to succeed. But every business owner—by committing private capital to a business enterprise—is contributing to the national economy: they are buying goods and services, paying wages, paying taxes and they're supporting themselves. Even if someone started a new business and ran it for two years before closing down, they would have put more into the economy than most, they would have supported themselves and their family, and into the bargain they would have sent eight business activity statements and payments to the Australian Taxation Office, thereby helping the government in the job of collecting taxes.

Our employees do their bit, too. Australians are known around the world as hard workers and problem-solvers; Australian financial, management and legal people are employed in many countries because they throw themselves into challenges and are good at chasing outcomes.

One of the reasons I have always liked private business, and have always championed business owners, is that they just get on with it. They have no union, no political voice and no media muscle, yet they are the fabric of our economy. And the fabric works like this: the big wheels of major corporations and government only turn because the smaller wheels of privately owned business are turning first. The big numbers like GDP and employment are only made possible by millions of smaller numbers. And that means a nation filled with hard workers, grinders.

Of course, there are no guarantees with business ownership, no matter how hard you work. The Australian Bureau of Statistics reveals middling-to-low odds for success: of the 316 850 businesses launched during 2007–08 in Australia, 71.5 per cent were still operating in June 2009, and less than half (48.6 per cent) were still operating as of June 2011.

In terms of turnover, you can accept that 13 000–16 000 privately owned businesses each year either 'enter' the market, or exit. These are not all distressed enterprises: some are wound up owing nothing; others are in the insolvency system.

Business owners are not the only ones who work hard for their success. There are millions of Australians employed in corporations, medium-sized companies and government who face similar stresses as their self-employed counterparts. Many of these people work together with business owners who run law firms, consultancies, contractors.

Successful employees, in my experience, also face fear and uncertainty, fatigue and the ever-present danger of burnout. Many of them have similar pressures associated with business ownership thrust on them via bonuses and project-completion incentives. The employment structure has changed enormously in the past twenty years, from a pyramid-shaped hierarchy of reporting to a more radial model, where the executive leadership sits at the hub of the wheel and at the end of each spoke is a management team that executes policy and strategy.

Law firms and accounting firms have always followed this model (small teams working on milestone-defined projects and reporting to the executive team) but nowadays just about anyone who wants to move upwards and make a name for themselves in the corporate or government world has to have first led one of these project-based teams and have done so within budget and to the brief. So these modern ambitious employees actually take on as much stress and risk as a business owner.

The reason I say that there are no secrets to business success is because it's all slog. Even students know it's the people who stay in the game, take the ups and the downs, who get through. It isn't a magic formula—no one gives you a degree. You earn it.

The funny thing about putting yourself through a test of mental and physical endurance—which is what much of life is—is that it makes you a happier person. I have been through all of these phases: university, a career in the professions and then a career as a business owner. It's all hard, it only works if you're relentless, and the sense of satisfaction and confidence you feel at the end is a precious thing, so long as you've been pursuing your purpose.

In my late twenties, when I was working as a chartered accountant at a law firm that specialised in structured finance for the oil exploration industry, I felt that my income would be better and my opportunities more interesting if I opened my own firm. So I did. I left with a couple of other lawyers and accountants and started my own business, and I worked harder over the next two and a half years than I had ever worked before. When you make a move like that—uprooting yourself from a good job and putting everything you own on the line, with many people wanting you to fail—you soon realise that there's only one way through: work. There are other aspects to a successful business that I'll get to later in the book: they include expertise, knowing what you're selling, knowing what you bring to the table and an ability to keep yourself from being crushed in the vortex of overwork. But the core of everything is work: hard, grinding, unglamorous work.

It was an ethic I took into my first foray into mortgage lending. It was the mid 1990s, and it had become possible for non-bank lenders to raise money from the capital markets and lend it as mortgages. I acquired a mortgage broker company in 1996 and convinced some of the guys to work with me, building a brand that would be known as Wizard Home Loans. We worked, and worked, and worked on that business, against the might of the banks and against the inertia of people conditioned to borrow from banks and building societies. It was hard but we stuck to it: loads of grind, some great investors and an attitude that we were not going to give up.

When we sold Wizard to GE Money in 2004, the business had $18 billion in assets and 230 branches in Australia and New Zealand. We had become the world's largest issuer of Australian residential mortgage-backed securities. It was an eight-year journey of pure toil.

I am now the executive chairman of Yellow Brick Road, a total financial solutions company, and I am working harder than ever.

So, it doesn't matter if you own a business or you're ambitious within someone else's. My message in this book is the same for both parties: forget about others telling you about success, because it will always be different for you; forget about secret methods and meditating towards riches; focus on working hard, being relentless and backing yourself for the best reason of all: your purpose.

CHAPTER 1

SUCCESS IS ATTITUDE

Success is not a place or a thing; success is the process of getting up every morning, putting in the work, dealing with the disappointments, striving for the wins and being able to say at the end of the year that you had more victories than defeats.

Success is the journey, success is the grind. Success is working at your purpose.

Think of the Olympics and Paralympics and the waves of athletes standing on podia, receiving gold, silver and bronze medals. Most people would call them successful because they've won a medal. But I don't see the success in these pieces of metal around the athletes' necks. And when you hear some of these medallists speak after the ceremonies, they admit that the victory was a 'relief', that it almost felt like an anticlimax after all the hard work. Some of them wish they could have had their coach on the podium. Why? Because the real success was the work, the striving, the pain—the early mornings, the parties missed, the lack of free time.

The real success was honouring their purpose. It always is.

If the Olympics were about real life, then the competitors would get an award for going and going and never giving up. They'd get medals for enduring the pain and the fear and the uncertainty and for getting back in the saddle every time they got thrown to the ground. Gold, silver, bronze? Forget it—life is about tough thinking, finding your purpose, honouring it and sticking to it.

People who do well in life, in my experience, share a similar attitude. If you take a look around and observe people who are successful in business, or have a good career in a corporation or the professions, or even are doing well at uni, they will all have the following things in common:

- They work hard.
- They don't give up.
- They know their purpose.

Look into the life and times of anyone who achieved something of note and you will find these elements at the base of their mode of living. They put in long hours, they never give up and they know exactly why they are doing what they are doing. Anything worth having is worth working for; anything worth achieving was never achieved by someone who gave up; and without a sense of purpose, the hard work and commitment is hard to sustain.

From the outside, this attitude is fairly boring. In fact, you will often find that the non-business media highlights the personal foibles and the lavish lifestyles of people who operate like this because the truth of how they live might not be that interesting.

Because, what time that business owners don't give to their business and professional endeavours, they give to their family and friends.

However, their success is presented as glimpses of 'wealth': Rich Lists, mansions, luxury yachts and family squabbles over lots of money. But these are the physical manifestations of the success. They are not success in itself.

Rupert Murdoch is not famous for having a lavish lifestyle. He's famous for his long days, his indefatigable approach to his business and his diamond-like clarity about what he's trying to achieve. Aristotle Onassis was the world's most powerful shipping magnate and his family lived in great luxury. But Onassis himself was renowned for being able to outwork any of his employees, never giving up and never wavering from his goal. Gina Rinehart, the world's wealthiest woman, is an example of the three qualities I ascribe to successful people, yet journalists prefer to write about her squabbles with her children over money. I don't see a clash over money—I see a hard-working, driven person finding it difficult to empathise with people who perhaps don't share her values.

The list could go on: Kerry Packer, Warren Buffet, Clint Eastwood, David Attenborough, Richard Branson, Robert Menzies, Jack Welsh, Muhammad Ali. For all of them, success comes with hard work, commitment and purpose.

THE RIGHT ATTITUDE

There are two ways to see this three-part foundation of success; it either annoys you, or you get it. Unfortunately, there are not too many shades of grey on this topic. There was a time in my early thirties when I'd started a professional services firm and I'd become involved in property developing, apartment buildings mainly. I was doing well by most counts but it had occurred to me that I seemed to work in fits and bursts. I could be quite complacent or relaxed for several weeks and when something need to be done, when money needed to be found, I'd erupt into a ball of energy and pursue my mission with a do-or-die intensity. As I realised how much I could get done in these bursts of energy, I began asking myself what I could achieve if I kept myself motivated and on the ball all the time. I switched to this mode—always hungry, always in a hurry—and set about doing everything from that time forth with a sense of urgency. It was urgency that energised me and it is urgency that I have carried as a hallmark of my business style ever since. Everyone has a signature mood that motivates them and allows them to bring an effective attitude to their business. For me, this turnaround crystallised the importance of hard work, never giving up and having a purpose.

I'm going to assume that anyone who's read this far understands what is being said and wants to hear more. Frankly, if you want to achieve your goals and you are lazy, you give up easily or you have no sense of purpose, then you might be relying on luck or cheating. And I can't do much for you on that score.

All of the achievement I have seen or experienced myself has come from periods of exertion and fatigue, where self-doubt has gnawed and the simplest thing was to give up. Everyone who has achieved a goal will tell you this. Just like the Olympic medallist, the glory at the end is simply the point where you can totally relax and give yourself a quick pat on the back. The actual success was the slog, and it was the ability to stay in the fight, not give up and constantly recall the purpose of the fight that was the real demarcation between success and failure, or between just making it and making a great job of it.

Which means that it's your attitude which keeps you going. A strong attitude is necessary for a number of reasons, including the following:

- **Taking responsibility**—If you get out of bed every morning with an attitude of hard work, resolution and a sense of purpose, you are accepting responsibility for how you walk in the world. I'm not talking about *control*, which too many people seek and become anxious when they can't achieve. I'm talking about the old-fashioned concept of taking responsibility for your own actions, which, in practical terms, begins with your mindset and your attitude. In fact, this is the ultimate act of self-responsibility: to create an attitude of your own making that you carry in everything you do.

- **Having perspective**—One of the most distracting results of living in such a media-infused world is the number of ideas thrust upon you that are so huge they are both well beyond your control while also being incredibly frightening. The global financial crisis is still being held over our heads for all sorts of government policies and corporate underperformance, yet it's too big and remote to have any control over. To concern yourself with this is to become anxious about lack of control, when you could just as easily be focusing on what you can take responsibility for: your work ethic, your resolution, your purpose. When you accept responsibility for these personal attitudes, you get things into perspective and waste less of your time being anxious about the things you can't control.

- **Dealing with change**—People who focus on their own personal attitude, and take responsibility for it, retain one massive advantage over those who don't: they can respond to change rather than being a victim of it. Being a steadfast person does not mean being inflexible. It means you retain strength where you can control it—in yourself—allowing you to deal with change, which in business and in life is constant.
- **Being active**—People who give up easily inevitably accept a passive role in their own lives. I don't mean this in a judgemental way, but if you want to build a business, do well in a corporation or enhance your professional reputation, you should be aiming for an active approach rather than a passive acceptance. When you sign on for hard work, resolution and purpose, you can never take the passive road because you have constructed an active approach to everything you do.
- **Inspiring others**—Most people who set out to make the best of themselves at some point have to take on the mantle of leadership. Whether you want to build a successful business, do a great job of bringing up your kids, or move up in a corporation, you will be asked to lead. When that time comes, you might like the role or hate it. Regardless of what you feel about leading a team, you will need to have the capacity to inspire better performances, to encourage people to move beyond their fears and to instil a sense of indefatigability. You will not be able to do this if you don't have the right attitude.
- **Taking ownership**—When you approach your life with hard work, commitment and purpose, you own it all: your mistakes and your triumphs, the good decisions and the bad. All successful people take ownership of their fortunes at

this basic level: it's like a marriage, because you sign on for better or worse. When you meet someone who is harsher on themselves for their own mistakes than anyone else could be, you know you are dealing with the right attitude.

One of the things not taught in the motivation seminars or the get-rich expos is what happens when things are not working so well in your business or the business you are working in. Because business operates in a dynamic environment, there are just as many ups as downs. And for every huge victory there is going to be a near wash-out. It happens to all of us. And it's when the tough times come around that motivational thinking seems more like wishful thinking.

Getting through the hard times is not a secret formula: it's about mental strength, remembering why you're doing this and being prepared to grind it out. Look at Rupert Murdoch, a man who has built so much yet has also gone through some terrible downturns and made some very risky, not always successful, deals. He keeps turning up, he doesn't get defeated, he's relentless and he doesn't complain. Maybe you can't be Rupert Murdoch, but you can practise mental strength and commitment to your business.

If you're still not convinced, try seeing it this way: one man goes out, creates a shoeshine business in a railway station and gets caught in the global financial crisis. Another man sets up a shoeshine stand in the same railway station. Both have the same income and outgoings; both are hit by a recession, when commuters are less likely to have their shoes shined on their way to work. But the first guy doesn't see the point of working hard when he doesn't really know what he's working for. It's all too hard, so he gives up.

The other guy knows why he's doing this and so he's prepared to keep working hard and never give up—he keeps going.

A year after the recession starts, the first guy has gone out of business and the guy who doesn't give up is working as hard as ever because he now has all the business coming through the railway station. And business is improving as the recession slowly lessens its grip and commuters are more confident again. After two years, he's employed someone at the first shoe shine stand and he's starting another business elsewhere.

This illustration of a good attitude is not complex yet it's the building block of just about every high-achieving person I can think of. And I'm not just talking about business owners: sports people, movie stars, singers, politicians and high-level employees all have this attitude. As do good parents and those people who commit time and effort to their communities and charities.

If nothing else, a good attitude will get you noticed and accepted by others with the same outlook. I have employed thousands of people in my career and taken on hundreds of franchisees as business partners in my financial services ventures. I have also invested in entrepreneurial companies and taken on investors in my own companies. So I know what I'm looking for at the first hurdle—even before expertise, education and prior experience. I'm looking for a person who has a good attitude because I know that when the business cycle turns and things don't go according to plan, it's people with this attitude who I can rely on and who take responsibility for their own actions.

So whether you own a business or you want to buy one, or you work as an employee or you're looking for a new job, this is what it takes: an attitude of hard work, commitment and purpose.

CHAPTER 2

PUTTING IN THE HARD WORK

A typical day for me goes like this: rise at 5.30 a.m., spend an hour reading online news services. On some mornings I exercise: walking, running, yoga or boxing. I usually sit down for a coffee around 7.30 a.m. at a café, where I read the *Sydney Morning Herald* and the *Australian Financial Review*. I'm at my office by 8.30 a.m. and I work until 6 p.m. On the days I don't exercise in the early morning, I do it in the afternoon or early evening.

Many of my social commitments are also business meetings and usually I review reports, notes from franchisees and other corporate correspondence after the evening meal, at my home office. This is where I have my ideas to follow up the next day, so I send emails and texts to prompt folks to get back to me in the morning. I'm in bed around midnight.

When I'm on the road, talking to investors and partners, or visiting the Yellow Brick Road (YBR) branches around Australia,

I cram five or six meetings into a day and get by on four hours sleep. I handle the pressures of travel by staying within the time limits of wherever I land, which means if I fly back into Sydney at 1 p.m., I will go straight to the office and work for the rest of the day; I don't think it's appropriate to ask a certain work ethic from my employees while I'm having an afternoon nap. If my flight gets into Perth, Singapore or Mumbai at 1 a.m., I will do my meetings and appointments in line with their working day.

I normally work six days a week, but when I travel I work every day to shorten the time I spend away.

This is not a moral position. This is what it takes to achieve what I want to achieve. And like anyone who lives like this, I become tired—sometimes exhausted—and later in the book I will share some tips about how to manage this. However, I put in the hours because this is my foundation, the absolute starting point. When I think about what it takes to build a business and do so with more good results than bad, this is where it starts: hard work.

•

Because of the career decisions I have made in my life—starting in the professions, moving into property investment and then into building financial services businesses—I have experienced a sort of two-track existence. On the one hand, I have worked with some people of great expertise and intelligence who have taught me, mentored me, invested with me and helped me to gain financial success; and, at the same time, I have become a person who is approached for advice on business, ideas and financial strategy.

Those who approach me for advice fall into two camps: people who have spent 10–15 successful years as an employee and now want to start or buy a business; and people who are in business but things aren't going as well as they'd like.

I invariably disappoint those who approach me for advice because I start with a question: 'How hard are you working?' or 'What sort of hours are you putting in each week?' or 'Are you giving it everything?' or even, 'How hard are your rivals working?'

This might sound like a simplistic approach to what are complex problems. But I don't believe I have ever seen a good career or a successful business which does not have hard work at its core. I'm always open to the idea that I'm wrong, but I'm yet to meet a successful business owner who can't get out of bed in the morning, and I have never met a senior partner in a law firm who did a regulation 40-hour week.

I think this is an important point to make early in this book, because there's a lot of details, tricks and insights that I want to reveal later. But the starting point of any discussion of what it takes to get where you want be has to be work—hard work, long hours, sacrifice, compromises and trade-offs.

This is important from several perspectives. Firstly, many people who have ground it out in the corporate world see owning their own business as a chance to take it easy, have a 'lifestyle', be more flexible in their working hours. This idea that the grass is greener and hours shorter on the other side of the fence is a mistake and in fact it works in the opposite direction in just about every private business I have ever heard of. Secondly, many people who parachute out of the corporate and professional worlds see themselves almost exclusively in terms of the skills and expertise they bring to the table: so the former corporate senior manager joins a technology start-up business, and she sees her involvement through the lens of what she knows rather than what she will have to put in. It isn't because she's lazy, it's because she has been used to having her expertise supported by the corporation's administrative staff. She's never had to lean on a client to pay their bill or argue with Telstra over an invoice. This will either create tensions with the other owners, or a culture shock for the corporate manager. Lastly, many people who are already in business are looking for ways to be more 'efficient' or 'work smarter', by which they usually mean they want to work less hours for more income. Here's the bad news: when improving or expanding your business, no one's going home early. It doesn't work like that.

The basic formula is this: you can have talent, education, training, experience, ideas, creativity, good connections, opportunity, luck and family backing. But if you don't have hard work underpinning all of these things, you have nothing. Well, nothing much.

Think of the Australian example of someone who, from the outside, seemed to be given a very good start in the world: Gina Rinehart. Rinehart inherited a mining company, Hancock Prospecting, from her father, Lang Hancock. When she was asked by ABC TV in 1976 what she thought of being a young millionairess, she responded: 'I know that I've got an awful lot of work to do so that I can carry on the work my father has been doing.'

Work! Gina Rinehart took over a successful company from her father in 1992 and could have sat on her dividend income for the rest of her life. But she didn't sit down. She worked on the business, expanded it and is now the richest person in Australia and the world's wealthiest woman, with assets of around $29 billion.

Rupert Murdoch inherited Sir Keith Murdoch's newspaper company when he was 22 years old. The company owned one paper, the *Adelaide News*. He has built that company into a conglomerate that owns Fox News Channel, Fox Studios, BSkyB, *The Wall Street Journal, The New York Post, The Australian* newspaper and HarperCollins publishers, as well as about 150 newspapers around the world and considerable media and entertainment assets in Latin America. He is worth more than $7 billion.

Murdoch has a famous work ethic. He told the select committee in the British Parliament in July 2012: 'I work a ten- or twelve-hour day.' He's 82 years old.

One of the political icons of my generation, former British prime minister Margaret Thatcher, also had a famous work ethic. The story I like is where she's working as a taxation lawyer, having failed in her attempt to become one of the youngest Conservative members of parliament. Six months after giving birth to her twins, she passed the bar exam. When she finally entered politics, she transformed the British and global governmental approach to economics and fiscal management, and she worked so hard that she could get by on a few hours sleep. She said: 'Look at a day when you are supremely satisfied at the end. It's not a day when you lounge around doing nothing; it's a day you've had everything to do and you've done it' (Goodreads.com, 'Margaret Thatcher Quotes', unattributed).

So the starting point is always hard work. But the formula has to be hard work plus. That is, I can bring my creativity and my experience to a project but they only count where they are joined to hard work. Same with education, connections or opportunity. Any of these things without hard work is almost irrelevant. As the cliché tells us, the world is filled with talented underachievers.

I see hard work in similar terms to how scientists see carbon: carbon is the chemical basis for all known life. It forms more compounds than any other known thing. Hard work is the carbon of success. It is the basis, the thing to which everything else has to join.

WHEN WORK MAKES A DIFFERENCE

Let's look at how this works in practice. Say you decide to end your days as an employee and you want to start a café, selling coffee and cakes in a trendy part of town. You look around, go to the other cafés in the neighbourhood, work out how much you can charge for a cup of coffee. You work backwards from the coffee price—and your margin per cup—and realise that you can either buy a café at the industry valuation of 2 × annual net earnings (revenues minus costs), or you can build your own café, and it will need at least six tables to make the kind of money you want to make. It seems to make perfect sense until the day comes when you realise that other café owners in the area have higher valuations because they are making more money.

You look closer at how the café that was sold for much more than yours is valued. It sells the same coffee, it serves the same cakes and cookies, and it seems to have similar traffic levels. But one thing is different: the owner of the other café opens at 7 a.m. and closes at 7 p.m., whereas you open at 8 a.m. and close at 4 p.m.

The other guy puts in more hours. The other guy is making more sacrifices. The other guy's café is worth $100 000 more than yours. The other guy is doing what it takes, and what it takes is hard work.

This works in the professions, too. You can start in a law firm on the same day as another woman; you both have good law degrees, have both done summer clerking at the firm, and have started on the same salary and seniority. But then she moves up faster than you, her billings get bigger, she gets thrown bigger clients and more work, and, before you know it, she's a partner and you're an associate.

What happened? Look closer. Does she start before you? Does she leave after you? Does she put her hand up for more work, when you're shirking? Do you occasionally get phone calls from her on a Saturday, asking where a file is? She's in the office, working!

She's no smarter than you and you both had the same opportunity. But she's investing hard work into her career and it's repaying her with higher billings, bigger clients, more seniority—and more salary.

It's the same for teachers, doctors, police detectives and landscape gardeners: they may all be good at their jobs, but the successful ones are those who work harder than the others.

It isn't that high-achieving people have less adversity or fewer headaches to counter in any week. They have the same mix of good and bad fortune as everyone. But because they put in the effort, they can mitigate the bad and accentuate the good.

So hard work is the building block. As you prepare for your new career or owning a business, perhaps reflect on where hard work fits into your life.

How hard can you work?

Invariably, when I have these discussions with people who ask my advice, the conversation comes around to 'How hard is *hard*?'

There's no straightforward answer to this. On normal weeks, I work 11-hour days Monday to Friday and perhaps five hours over the weekend. Let's say 60 hours. If something is happening, I will work 15-hour days, six days a week. Let's say more than 80 hours.

This is not a formula, it's what works for me. I like to start early. I like to work a standard office day, because not only do I want to stay close to the business but I like my managers to have access to me. And I like to make the most of the quieter time after I've eaten in the evening, when I can concentrate on corporate reports and correspondence that I couldn't get to during the day. I also use this time to watch the business shows on cable TV, which again can trigger ideas or make me remember something.

For me, this kind of schedule isn't onerous; in fact, I find that by working a lot of hours I can devote different parts of my responsibilities to certain times: taking in information in the morning; managing and being a leader through the day; reflecting and reviewing at night.

I know people in business who do less than this, and I know people who do more, especially when they have international interests and have their conference calls at night. I also take on more stress and financial overheads than many business owners and so I need a long working day just to get to everything I need to get to. Living like this is not for everyone. However, achieving in business is about operating to your full potential and part of that potential has to include the sheer quantum of working hours you can put in. No, it's not fair, especially if you're an ambitious woman with young kids, or if you have personal responsibilities which don't allow you to travel, or even if you live in the regions where there actually isn't enough work for a 12-hour day, whether you want to or not.

But all of these restrictions aside, as you assess your suitability for owning a business or jumping into a new career, start with your work ethic: how hard can *you* work?

Before changing careers or buying a business, I suggest you start with an honest appraisal of what kind of hours you can put in. You might be limited in terms of what you can do because of family commitments. If you have stress-related medical conditions, you should assess what hours are required from your new venture, and make your decisions accordingly. You should always be honest about how your metabolism works: if you're slow to wake and hate getting out of bed, then you probably shouldn't buy a bakery, a butcher's shop or a florist. They can be up and about at 4.30 in the morning. If you find it hard to stay awake late at night, don't own a nightclub, a restaurant or a security business.

If the metabolism argument is a factor for you, or if the idea of working long hours is unrealistic, then start from the other end: match who you are to the type of business you want to run.

There are many businesses out there—retail, franchises, services companies—where the hours are either contained or can be adjusted to suit personal preferences. There are also niches in the professions where, if you can show a deep expertise in a certain discipline, you may be able to increase your revenue without doing the long hours. But that's a big *maybe*, and you'll still eventually be knocked off by the person who can work twice as hard.

So, whether you're planning to own a business, or thinking about a new assault on a corporate or professional career, start with hard work. Every high-achieving person started at the same place.

CHAPTER 3

BEING RELENTLESS

So you've learned how to work hard? Okay, now do it again. And again. And again . . . And if it doesn't work out, keep trying.

Most of the important concepts are not complicated, and this is one of them. Even if all things are equal and you have the same education, opportunity and financial books as your rivals; even if the economic climate is bad for you and all your competitors; even if no one is making much money and every one of your professional peers is talking about jumping ship and going to another industry; even in this scenario, where there is no extra margin or secret way to riches being exploited by any of you, this is the rule: *The winner is the guy who doesn't give up.*

This doesn't mean you keep on keeping on when sales are strong and revenues are healthy and everything is blue sky. Anyone can do that. Being relentless means you approach a day of troubles and failures with the same energy with which you approach successes and good news. Persistence means you focus on what could be rather than what just happened. It isn't that bad things don't happen to persistent people, it's more that they find a way to keep going and stay focused on the ultimate goal.

In my twenties I lived around Rushcutters Bay, in Sydney's Eastern Suburbs, and I'd go drinking with a mate of mine; let's call him Bill. Bill wasn't very big or very strong; he was medium height, average build and was a fairly easygoing chap. One night, he ended up in a blue with someone we knew by reputation, a heavy-set bloke who was a good street fighter.

Bill lost the blue and the next time I saw him, he told me he wasn't going to settle for that crap; so he went to the street fighter's house and called him out. Bill lost again. This went on for a week and people were scared for Bill because he kept getting beaten up. But Bill didn't like this street fighter's style—he thought he was a bully and wanted to beat him. Finally, after a week of beatings, Bill got it over the bully and won. Whereupon the street fighter gave up—he handed it to Bill and said that was it, no more.

And that was it. The persistent average guy beat the talented, unmotivated guy. But in order to get his win, Bill had to take many beatings. In order to find success he had to endure failure and not give up.

Stories like this abound in our lives: team-mates who match-up to tougher opponents because they won't give in; people who end up married to the person they're in love with because they don't give up; people who are no smarter than their classmates but come through with great exam results because they never stopped trying.

Persistence, in my opinion, is a most undervalued virtue. It is an attribute that can trump intellect, talent and experience because any of these other routes to victory can be undermined by a lack of ticker, or simply a lack of motivation. But someone who's relentless never gives up. They stay in the fight, even when—like Bill—they're being beaten by someone who outclasses them. They keep trying when many would be demoralised and even embarrassed. They keep coming back in spite of the bruises and the blood and the tears, and they are there at the end, where it counts.

I have spent many years being a sports fan, and what I like best in my two favourite sports—rugby league and boxing—is the sight of the combatant who never gives up. When I was growing up in Punchbowl, a tough neighbourhood in Sydney's west, rugby league and boxing were the sports we followed and the nature of those sports is that it's virtually impossible to have success at even a low level if your heart's not in it.

So I gravitated towards footy heroes like Tommy Raudonikis and boxing heroes such as Jeff Fenech. Neither of them were flashy. Neither were gifted with being the biggest, the fastest or the most talented. They weren't charismatic like Muhammad Ali, and they weren't freakishly athletic like Björn Borg. But they were tenacious, hard-working and incapable of quitting.

Raudonikis was a scrum half for the Western Suburbs Magpies during the 1970s, a time when rugby league was a sport for physically hard people. He captained New South Wales and Australia and would later coach the Blues in State of Origin.

Jeff Fenech became a world champion in three weight divisions after turning pro following the 1984 Olympic Games. He retired with a record of 28 wins, three losses, one draw and 21 knockouts.

I looked up to these people not because of their fame or because they won most of the time, but because they represented a relentless attitude. They were never beaten, even when they were beaten. For me this attitude was reinforced both at home—by my parents—and at my high school, LaSalle Catholic College Bankstown (Benilde High), which also educated former prime minister Paul Keating. This school has the official motto of 'Commitment, Confidence, Success', but its real motto was 'Never, Ever, Give Up'.

Many things were excused at Benilde, but not the desire to quit.

I am in debt to these influences in my life because, having graduated from the University of New South Wales with my Bachelor of Commerce in 1973, I entered straight into a world of professional services firms where the pressure was high and many people from the graduate intakes dropped out to pursue careers with more stable hours and less demands. I managed to stick it out in the accounting/law firm I worked at, which was the best thing I could have done. It taught me the value of perseverance and stamina and gave me an insight into the habits of some very smart and wealthy people.

From the early days I was funnelled towards the business of structuring finance solutions for oil and gas explorers, who needed to juggle debt with equity via convertible notes and debentures. It was a world where companies were forever having to rejig these financial arrangements and some of the documents and valuations we'd put together for banks and investors would have to be finished overnight. I saw these people up close and worked through the night with many of them in order to meet bank and investor deadlines.

But there were other people who did their 'working' hours and then went home—smart, educated people who always had to be somewhere else—people who would start looking at their watches at 7 p.m. when they knew we needed a draft by 10 o'clock in the morning. Let's not be judgemental about this, because not everyone is motivated by their work and not everyone wants to keep going even when they are tired and meeting a deadline seems hopeless.

However, even if we're not being judgemental, let's acknowledge this: persistence is not only an under-rewarded virtue, it's almost an entry requirement for people who want to get ahead. If you want to excel in your business, or you want to push to the top of your corporation or your firm, you will need to foster a relentless attitude. There are some very good psychological arguments behind what I am saying, but I can put it most simply by emphasising this—someone has to be the last man standing, and if it's not you, then it's someone else.

The business world attracts some highly motivated, relentless people and these people will put in the extra hours, they will find more things to improve, they will make the extra phone calls, they will work the weekends and meet the impossible deadlines.

I'm not confining this observation to people who have had to work their way up from 'nothing'. People say this of me, but I think I was given the greatest gift: a work ethic and a reluctance to quit. It's something I share with other people, some of whom came from great privilege. James Packer inherited a business empire worth around $4 billion from his father, Kerry. But he has been quoted as saying that the greatest lesson from his father was persistence: 'Dad was an amazing man and I think that he had a capacity to keep going and be very determined about things when he needed to be. That was a real lesson. I don't think that life for any of us is a one-way road. But just keep going' (James Thomson, *Packer on Casinos, Kerry*, Crikey.com, 26 October 2012).

DEVELOPING PERSEVERANCE

The ability to persevere in your business dealings is an asset that you can develop and improve on. While many high achievers are born with a stubborn streak—and are energised by toil—perseverance is also something that can be learned and built up. Here are some suggestions about how to develop perseverance.

SET ACHIEVABLE TIMELINES

You can develop persistence by adjusting the timelines on your goals. Rather than set a target for the year, set it for the week. If you own a café, don't aim to increase coffee sales over a year, but aim instead to achieve your desired increase next week. Train your persistence by committing to shorter schedules. Train yourself to go after the shorter goals, and train yourself to expect that you'll pursue them. As you achieve these goals, you can extend your horizon and go after longer-term goals.

SIZE MATTERS

Just as you reduce the length of time you have to persist, also reduce the quantum of the increase you are aiming for. Rather than setting yourself the task of increasing your coffee sales by 50 per cent in a year, start by aiming for an increase of 50 cups in a week. It's like swimming: you don't peel off 50 fast laps the first time you go to the pool. You build your stamina with repetition, so what was impossible six months ago is something you now do several times a week. Set a small increment of improvement, and don't stop until you achieve it. And make this a habit.

LEARN FROM FAILURE

As you reduce the timeframe of your goals to, say, a week, try a popular intellectual exercise of converting a 'failure' into a 'lesson'. If you have had problems with managing disappointment in the past, and your instinct is to give up when things get sticky, it's probably because setbacks and stumbles have overwhelmed you. If this is the case, try looking at your inability to sell 50 extra cups of coffee in a week not as failure, but as a free lesson: What did you learn? What can you do differently next week? Think it through, find the lesson and then set a new goal.

LOOK AT THE NEXT STEP

Learn the habit of planning what has to happen differently next week; management consultants call it 'continuous improvement'. I call it my state of mind where I'm just a little paranoiac. It goes like this: rather than thinking of immediate setbacks being the end of your career or business, think always in terms of a horizon you're aiming for and what you can change to improve things at that time. Persistent people believe that by staying in the fight, they can dictate the outcome. Do what they do—don't be trapped in the negative moment; push out the timeframe instead.

ASK QUESTIONS

Creating a persistent and relentless approach might be as simple as making one thing a very strong habit. For me, it's questions. In my own businesses, I have an endless routine of self-questioning and also questioning of staff, advisers and customers. It's a relentless process that doesn't stop with the business plan and isn't confined to weekly management meetings. Every day I question business strategy and operations, even if sometimes it's just looking at small assumptions and wondering if they are relevant now or if they could be improved. Other times, I read something in the newspapers that affects my business—interest rates, financial regulation, superannuation rules—and it can trigger a question that I might pursue for several days until I am satisfied with the answer. Or maybe I'm prompted by an external adviser making a comment or a customer with a query. I travel extensively because the franchisees for Yellow Brick Road are located around Australia and I like to see them face to face and ask them about the business, the customers, the trends. I find this valuable because not only does it knit the far-flung components of my company together, but it gives me coal-face market research. And if you're in business and you're not interested in the market, then you won't be in business for long.

Relentless questioning does not mean you don't know what you're doing—it means you want to know your market. The business media used to make fun of Gerry Harvey's penchant for stopping at any Harvey Norman retail outlet he was driving past and walking in for a chat with whoever was around: customers, staff, suppliers. I don't see anything eccentric about Harvey's habits.

HARDEN UP

The other way to achieve a 'learned' sense of persistence is to rethink the universe in which you operate: business is hard, so the hard succeed. You think you're the only one who deals with sales slumps, earnings downgrades, tax problems? Take these words of advice from Australian mogul, Rupert Murdoch: 'You just gotta learn to take it. You just gotta shrug it off' (Quoteswise.com, 'Rupert Murdoch Quotes', unattributed).

•

Hard work and a relentless commitment to what you're doing is what it takes to be successful. All successful people have a work ethic which they apply every day of their lives. Both work and persistence can be learned and practiced, and they can be made into personal as well as business virtues by anyone who wants to adopt them. But both of these vital elements are made so much more powerful when they are helped along by the key to it all: purpose.

CHAPTER 4

KNOW YOUR PURPOSE

There was a time in the expansion days of my mortgage venture, Wizard Home Loans, when the organisation needed to grow from a largely Sydney–Brisbane–Melbourne operation, with 25 branches, and into an Australasian operation with at least 150 branches and a big advertising and marketing campaign behind it. It eventually grew to 230 branches.

It wasn't the kind of corporate expansion that you ask the banks to fund with a loan, because my business model was to compete with the banks by offering lower priced and better mortgage products. So I needed to get a large investor into the business who could bring not only money but also some influence and experience.

Through a series of social connections, I managed to find myself in front of a very wealthy, very powerful person who also had a tonne of experience and acumen when it came to building businesses. I talked about my model and the business, the size of the Australian home loan market and the fact that even though Australian borrowers were the lowest risk in the world, the Aussie banks were charging them exorbitant interest rates. In other words, the incumbents were overcharging sure-bet borrowers, and even a 2 or 3 per cent bite out of this market was worth billions.

The investor heard me out, asked some very astute questions and told me that if Wizard really wanted to own 3 per cent of the Australian mortgage market, the company would have to have its own funding mechanism via the capital markets and not be reliant on the banks (he was proved right). But the kicker was this: he told me that if he was going to invest the kind of money I was asking for—over $25 million—I had to have pain in the game, that he wasn't going to just give me some Monopoly money to play with. He wanted me to hurt if the thing didn't work—he thought that would make us more like partners. And then he said it: 'Come back when you've got seven million dollars to put into this business, then I'll invest.'

At that time there were other people who might have been interested in a stake in Wizard, but none with the influence, reach and business brain of the person I'd targeted. I wanted him as a partner as much as I wanted his money. At the same time, most of the capital I could lay my hands on myself had already been invested into getting Wizard to where it was. So I had to drop everything, and for almost a month I did nothing but find the money to put into Wizard. I travelled throughout Europe in a blur, talking to investors, funds and banks until I had my money. It was stressful and exhausting.

When I arrived back in Sydney, I had the money and, true to his word, my investor joined me in the business. That happened in 1999. In 2004, we sold Wizard to GE Money for $500 million and our investor was returned more than $100 million. Not bad for a five-year investment.

When I look back on that phase of my life—I was 43—I see hard work and I see a relentless approach to what I was doing. But I see something else, something that held everything together. I had purpose. I knew what it was I was trying to achieve, I knew why it was important and I knew my part in the scheme of the whole thing. I felt aligned with the goal and I loved the pursuit and the fight, even as I became exhausted on that journey through Europe.

WHAT IS PURPOSE?

In my lifetime, some words have picked up connotations they shouldn't have, and 'purpose' is one of them. For me, purpose is real—it's the compass you keep with you, that reminds you of what direction you are supposed to be going in. It is not a new-age concept or a religious idea. It's the reason you're working so hard, the reason you're always stressed and tired. Your purpose is the guidance system on the guided missile. Without it you're a fast, dangerous projectile who could land anywhere and either hurt yourself or someone else.

Purpose doesn't immunise you from the pain. It doesn't stop you making mistakes. But purpose is the thing you need to constantly bring the stress and the fear back into perspective. Purpose is like the rock under the foundation, which holds up the building. You don't see it but without it the whole building would collapse.

Purpose performs this function. I get out of bed every morning at 5.30—I have to know why I'm doing that; I have to know why I'm at work for ten or eleven hours a day and why I'm still sending emails at 11 p.m., or why I'm exhausting myself on a business trip.

I have to know why, and I believe you do, too.

When people want to talk to me about their businesses, their ideas and careers, invariably the root of their confusion or their indecisiveness comes back to either a lack of purpose or an inability to articulate their purpose. Some people are not pursuing their purpose in life and in business, and this is a problem which causes many other issues in terms of health, marriage and interaction with their kids. Equally self-undermining is the person who knows he has a purpose, but cannot articulate it. In fact, the inability to articulate your reasons for work can be more frustrating than not having any reason in the first place.

All the most successful people I have met are very clear about their purpose. They may not write it on a wall and call it a mission statement, and they may not discuss it with people they've just met. But it is there nonetheless. It is a small fire burning inside them, the ultimate reference point that is beyond the spreadsheets and the monthly figures. They have a purpose—they have a reason.

Can you learn this? I believe you can, but it can only be taught by you, to you. Purpose cannot be laid out in a list of 'missions' that are tacked onto the wall of the staff kitchen area. I am amazed that so many organisations do this, because purpose is personal—that's where its power comes from. Also, purpose is not a top-down exercise driven by senior managers: purpose is revealed by people being very honest with themselves, when they ask such basic questions like the ones I'm about to ask you now.

WHY?

One of the most powerful tools is the ability to articulate why you are doing what you are doing. The person who has the guts to ask themselves 'Why?' at least once a week, and be totally honest with themselves about the answer, is already twenty steps ahead of their smarter, more experienced rival.

Every journey needs a starting point, and this should be it for anyone who wants to own a business or rise in a competitive field. It's especially important in an economy where people will have two or three careers in their lifetime: smart people can no longer 'set and forget' their career. Each shift will come with a change in skills, culture, education and objectives, and with each of these career shifts will come the need to re-evaluate the 'why' behind the job.

So why do so many ambitious people avoid this sort of questioning? Why do they set it aside or ridicule those who have realised the power of it? It's not as if the crisis of 'Why?' isn't rife in most workplaces; I'm going to guess that the majority of people, at very stressful points in their working lives have turned to a friend or workmate and asked, 'Why the hell am I doing this?'

It's actually an excellent question, and part of its usefulness is that it's the question we ask when we're at our wit's end. Which means it's one of those basic questions that gnaws at us. So why let it go? In my experience—as a person who has been very frustrated and asked this question many times—the more you confront this question and make yourself answer it, the easier it is to establish your purpose. And when you establish your purpose you start to align your hard work with what it is you're trying to achieve and what you think is important. And when you do this, you can work harder and remove the temptation to give up.

So many people work in a world of 'must': must finish the report, must meet with the client, must ring the bank. Every so often try 'Why?' and see where it takes you.

WHAT AM I DOING?

Many people who aim for the top in business, professions, corporations and government departments are people who see themselves in technical terms in the first place. They see their skills, their abilities, their experience or even—in extreme cases—their job title. So the person who buys a coffee shop, when asked what she's doing, will say, 'I own a coffee shop.' When pushed, she may admit that 'I sell coffee.' The ambitious publisher says, 'I'm a publisher.' When pushed, she may say, 'I sell books.'

These are technical descriptions describing a title, a product and a transaction.

Finding your purpose means finding a more honest alignment between yourself and the outside world, where you go a bit deeper. For the person who owns a garden centre, the answer could be, 'I provide the beautiful plants and expertise so that people can create a relaxing sanctuary in their home.' For the person who owns a coffee shop, the answer is, perhaps, 'I provide a warm, safe place where people can start their day with a hot drink in a relaxing environment.' For the publisher the answer might be, 'I'm sharing ideas with a community of readers.'

This is what I mean by, 'What are you doing?' I'm talking about getting down to the essence of what it is that you are *doing* in life, as opposed to what you *do* for a job. You are mired all day in the technical and pragmatic aspects of your occupation—you are allowed to take five minutes each week to remind yourself of the essence of the thing; you're allowed to dig down slightly and find the essential role you play as opposed to the technical actions you perform.

Purpose is really about aligning the real you with the practical world you inhabit. But how do humans do this when they are either reluctant to—or discouraged from—discovering what really makes them tick?

Many people I speak to become stressed because they feel as if they've been cut adrift of the whole point of it all. They're often people who repress their own self because they think this will make them a better employee or better business owner—they think this makes them cold to some of the existential aspects of their unhappiness. But it makes it impossible to align themselves. And in this sense, they feel adrift from their purpose. That's why they're so stressed, so tired and so physically run-down. They are not asking, 'Why?' and they are not asking, 'What am I doing?' And invariably, they are not asking, 'Who benefits?'

WHO BENEFITS?

Purpose doesn't have to be a goody-goody concept for it to be powerful. The television program *Breaking Bad* features a person who—faced with terminal illness and wanting to provide for his family before he goes—takes a job cooking methamphetamine.

What he is doing is not legal or honourable but I believe the reason audiences relate to him is that he knows why he's doing what he'd doing, and is constantly reminding himself. This is his driver, his engine.

One way to ensure you never lose sight of your purpose is to make yourself answer the question, 'Who benefits?' In a capitalist society, a large number of employees, and a majority of business owners, see the question of who benefits as entirely an issue of remuneration. In many respects the world is set up like this, and we all know people who seem to be driven by their income and nothing else. Are they happy? Do they feel they're missing something?

I think people who work hard usually have to do it for slightly broader reasons than just lining their own pockets. For some hard-working employees, the answer may lie in the photos of a spouse and kids that adorn their desk. People with a good-sized business might look out of their window and see twenty employees who are relying on their wages and superannuation, and who want a job next week. For someone else, the whole point of working hard is to enjoy the rewards: they might have a picture of a ski resort or a sports car tacked onto their office wall. I know people who have kept a set of golf clubs in their office to remind themselves of what they're working for.

It doesn't matter: the question of who benefits is not a test. No one from HR is looking over your shoulder, no one can decide if you're selfish, deluded or grandiose. It has to make sense to you. You have to know who benefits and you have to know if it's worth all the hard work. That's where you find your purpose, when you answer questions like this, to yourself.

Using purpose

Okay, so you're on your way to knowing who you are, because you interrogate yourself and answer the basic questions honestly. You get the hang of it and after a while it becomes second nature. But knowing yourself in an internal sense also has an external or practical dimension. And that is, how you use your purpose.

I see purpose as the alignment of your true self with your practical, occupational activities, between who you really are and what you actually do. It's as if what's truly important to you is expressed in your occupation or business. So, purpose includes the deeper, more emotional sides of you that are not necessarily known by others. And it also includes what you do.

People who are very lucky and hard-working often get to say that they don't mind the long hours and the stress of their business or their career, because they like what they're doing. I'm one of those lucky people. When I'm working hard and achieving there is no place I'd rather be than at work. People call me 'driven', but I don't think that's it.

I've chosen something I want to create, that reflects what I think is important for people: the desire to own the roof over your head, and the desire to be able to retire comfortably. That's what Yellow Brick Road does: whole-of-life financial advice that provides the best mortgage and the best strategy for building assets for retirement. I feel good when I'm providing these basics and making people feel more secure. It motivates me, along with all of the excitement of building a business.

There is also a classic type of purpose, when your professional self corresponds to what you like doing anyway: your professional accomplishment feeds your personality and your personality feeds your work life. You sometimes meet these people: the environmentally aware lawyer who works for Greenpeace; the footy-mad accountant who works for a football club; the petrol-head who's a mechanic on a professional racing car team.

Not everyone falls into this blessed group, but that's okay because there are other ways to get there and they can be fostered. For instance, many successful people express their purpose by applying their talent or skill. They may not feel that their skill is an accurate definition of their true selves, but they feel good in performing a difficult or tricky task for clients. This could include carpenters, lawyers, interior designers. Take your pick—they might not be living out a childhood fantasy, as such, but they certainly find their purpose in being able to do something of specific expertise that adds value to peoples' lives.

Another kind of purpose might entail doing what you have to do because it will get you somewhere else. So a coffee shop owner might work diligently building up her business for sale because she really wants to step up to a large restaurant or a pub. An accountant might be putting in the hard yards because he wants to stash away enough money to start his own firm. And so on.

Everyone needs a purpose, and different people come to it differently. Some people can only find it when they are away from their work, and others need to be immersed. But the fastest way I know to become clear about your purpose is to ask yourself the basic questions and then answer them with as much honesty as possible.

In your answer is the answer.

CHAPTER 5

WHAT IT TAKES

Getting your attitude right is an important precursor to starting a business or embarking on a professional challenge such as a new career or project. Without it you're not going to get far. So I always start with the basics, and they are hard work, being relentless and having purpose. But as you get closer to making a commitment about your next project, you're going to have to move beyond your attitude and mindset and ask yourself a bunch of practical questions. And it's best to sort out the answers to these questions *before* you start a new venture. They are:

- What do I want to achieve?
- How am I going to achieve this?
- Can I do what it takes to get there?

I like the process of self-questioning because it makes me respond to myself. It forces me to focus on central issues and resolve them. And even if in answering a question I raise other issues, that's okay because I turn those into questions and force myself to answer them. It can go on all day.

This system—called 'Socratic'—is powerful because it turns your mind to problem-solving. It's valuable in determining my purpose, as I have pointed out in the previous chapter. But it's also priceless for formulating the plan. And everyone needs a plan. If you rejig the questions you have to ask before throwing yourself into your new venture, they come out looking like this three-part system:

- goal
- strategy
- discipline.

It looks simple but I can tell you—as can many professionals who work with business owners—this essential first step is often overlooked. There are people with a goal and tonnes of discipline, but they don't have a strategy; there are people with pages of goals and strategy, but they don't have the discipline to execute; and, of course, there are highly strategic and disciplined people whose goals are so amorphous that it's unclear what they're trying to achieve.

There are consultants out there who will take your money and write you a business plan. However, what these people are usually doing is assessing the *external* issues in your venture: good consultants know that you have to craft your business planning to accommodate other people and forces. This is why a business plan accounts for what an investor, a customer, a buyer, a partner, a supplier and a bank wants to hear. I'll go into these external answers later on. But before you get into pleasing everyone else, you have to understand your own motivations, plans and actions.

So before worrying about what everyone else wants to hear, the questions of goal, strategy and discipline have to be addressed by you. If it helps to refer to them as 'where I want to be', 'how I'm going to get there' and 'the commitment to execute my plans', then say it this way. The point is to be very clear about what your expectations are of yourself.

I don't care if you don't write them down. You can keep them in your head, make them part of a daily conversation, stick them to your bathroom mirror or write them on the back of a beer coaster. But however you do it, when someone asks you about your goal, your strategy or your intention to see it through, you must have an answer.

When you launch into your project, you may not have thought about this, but this is what is happening: you are entering a market. You are not so different from a fishmonger or a greengrocer standing in the souk. You are supplying something and you are trying to match this with demand. The 'market' is the point where demand is met by supply, and a price is set. Business owners create this market every day when they supply goods or services, which meets demand.

You are always in a market and you are always supplying something to meet demand. To remain clear about what you're doing and how you're going about doing it, you need to have your goal, strategy and execution solid in your mind at all times.

Employees are not so different: they have a skill they supply, betting that there is demand, at a certain price. These people need to be as clear as business owners. When a prospective employer asks what your goals are, you don't want to be rolling your eyes and mumbling. If you're an entrepreneur and a venture capitalist asks you how you intend to meet your three-year goal, you'd better have something better than a shrug.

The three-part system of goal, strategy and discipline is my starting point, but there are many ways to get these steps wrong, which I'll go through.

GOAL

Excuse me if this seems obvious, but when you have seen as many business plans as I have, and spoken with as many ambitious people as I have, then you realise that even very smart people can't set goals.

What is a goal? A goal is the absolute starting point for your plan. Yes, you read that correctly: the goal is not the end point—the goal is the start. The goal informs the strategy and the goal dictates the discipline. All plans revolve around the goal. For instance, when I start a business, I imagine the position I wish to be in, which for me is a five-year plan at which point my business will be valued by the market at × amount, being valued at three times its earnings of Y.

This is simply how I do it, but I find it effective. I am very specific about the value the market attaches to my venture, at a point in time. So I believe in articulating the goal in market valuation terms. I need to be specific because everything I do to reach that goal will be structured backwards from that point. Therefore, the goal is the start, even if it is five years in the distance.

If you can't articulate your own goal, your strategy will not make a lot of sense. If you can't reduce the goal to a sentence, then you probably haven't convinced yourself. And if you can't convince yourself, then you'll have trouble convincing investors, partners, key personnel and banks. If you're going for a new job, you'd better believe what you're saying. If you don't believe it, why should an employer?

When you're setting your goals, the following things can go wrong:

- **Ambition**—Ambition is not a goal. To be famous, rich or successful are not goals. Even declaring that you want to be like Richard Branson is not a goal. Yet we often hear people offering up these ideas as what they're aiming for. If you tell an investor you want to be Richard Branson, he may wonder: 'If that's the case, what's wrong with who you are?' And if you tell a venture capitalist you want to be the next Jeff Bezos, he may well think: 'I don't want to know about the next Jeff Bezos, I want to hear about you.'

- **Vagueness**—Sometimes your goal doesn't really state what you're chasing. It better describes an idea rather than outlining an event. Rather than saying your goal is to be one of the best small courier companies in Melbourne, you could sharpen it to a specific action: for example, 'My goal is to win the 2015 Best Courier in Victoria award.' Being specific about your goal makes you specific about your planning and gets you focused.

- **Money**—Though some people disagree with me on this, I don't believe amassing lots of money is a good goal. Money can form part of a strategy. For example, you might want to aim to increase revenues by x per quarter. And money can also measure the goal. But simply creating an entire plan around a monetary result is usually not successful. Money is a form of exchange and it is one measure of success, but it doesn't work well as a goal unless hitched to a business outcome. I think valuations, earnings targets and equity amounts—which can all be reduced to money—are preferable to the goal of money in itself.

- **Value**—Rather than set a sum of money as your goal, concentrate on value. If you're building a business, set a goal around what sort of valuation a potential buyer will put on your business in three years time. Work around earnings multiples, or bolstering a certain revenue stream that the market wants, or pushing your marketing to a certain segment so you can say you 'own' a sought-after demographic. Think market value rather than money in your pocket. Think equity value, which is the surplus of assets over liabilities in your business. If you're going into a new career as an employee, don't think about your target salary—think about the demand you fulfil with your skills and work ethic. Think about the world you work in as a talent market, and try to improve where you sit on the demand curve. The salary is the cherry on top—it's a measure of success, not the goal.

- **Timeline**—I always set time constraints on my goals. It makes the goal more real and it allows more meaningful work with the planning. Sometimes when I see a business plan without a solid deadline, I assume the person behind it is looking for an escape hatch if things don't work out. And if that's the case, it isn't a goal—it's a wish.

- **Wish list**—Effective goal-setting does not entail a list of things you'd like to be or have. Goals are not a wishing well. I know I'm looking at a weak set of goals when it's a collection of sentences that start with, 'to be'. For instance, 'to be the best in my industry', 'to be the highest-selling café in New South Wales' or 'to be compared to Richard Branson'. Likewise, a list that includes 'to have a Ferrari' or 'to have an apartment on Bondi Beach' is not really goal-setting.

- **Change**—This may sound counter-intuitive, but it's easier to alter a business plan that has a specific goal than it is to alter a plan with an abstract goal. Why? Because a specific goal has required a specific plan, so altering means changing some of the variables in your calculations, to get to a new goal. But changing from one wishy-washy goal to another will probably require a complete reworking of the plan. It's worth thinking about this because every business plan needs change at some point. The tighter the goal, the easier it is to alter strategy when the need arises.

STRATEGY

At some point in the last ten years, 'strategy' became an overused and underappreciated word. It was trotted out to give an intellectual cover to mass sackings; it was used to excuse paying too much for overvalued dotcom businesses; it became the big alibi for meetings that went on all morning when they should have been over in half an hour. But strategy is a powerful tool and it is the crucial element of your planning because it's the practical road map of executing your intentions. And because it is crucial, strategy is often the weak point of a plan. Here are a few thoughts on getting your strategy right:

- **Keep it simple**—Just as the goal has to be specific, strategy has to be simple. I don't mean simplistic: I mean that you should be able to explain to a person with no prior knowledge of you or your industry how you intend to achieve your goals. Why? Because being clear means you understand it, and if you understand it, it's likely the strategy makes sense. If you can't explain the strategy to an outsider, then I would suspect it needs more work. It may be correct at its core and it may have some great ideas, but if it's confusing then it's not really strategy. Imagine being an army general laying out a battle plan. If your soldiers don't get it, it's a confused plan. The same goes for business owners and their strategies.
- **Narrative**—If the strategy seems a little convoluted, try rearranging it as a narrative. Imagine the strategy is a person taking steps towards the goal, and describe each step. Sometimes the confused strategy became that way because the writer tried to throw everything in at once and forgot to use chronology and priority. When in doubt, tell it like a story. And if you can't do that, grab a clean piece of paper and start again by listing the steps in point form.
- **Question**—Try examining your strategy with a question for every step you describe: 'How is this taking me closer to my goal?' This is a good exercise for when you've spent too long developing the strategy and it begins to waffle. Be honest

about making each step answer your question and you'll see it coming back into focus.

- **Know your goal**—Build your goal into the first sentence of your strategy. Constantly refer to it. Don't let the strategy become a shaggy dog story with a magical result at the end. Remember: the strategy is a road map for getting to your goal. It's not supposed to be literary or intellectual. The strategy serves the goal.

- **Back-up materials**—PowerPoint, spreadsheets and videos are all nice in their own context, but they are really support materials designed to inform the secondary players in your strategy, such as employees, investors, major suppliers, etc. This filigree is okay for marketing purposes, so long as you know that's what you're doing. But a strategy is not about support material or marketing, it's a tool and it needs to be simple and unadorned.

- **Keep it short**—The strategy sections of most business plans I have written have been not much more than two pages. A good plan can be boiled down to key ingredients and the most important measurements. It doesn't have to be a 50-page essay. It has to be a battle plan which guides you—and possibly an investor or key employees—towards a goal.

- **Executable**—Don't think that by aiming too high you are creating a greater chance that you will succeed. I know about these reach-for-the stars theories and they often make their way into business plans. As far as I'm concerned, the strategy document is like an architect's plans—it's a blueprint for execution. It is no place for wish lists or grandiose delusions. The same goes for employees. If your goal is to enter a major bank and work your way up to being CFO, don't make it your strategy to be offered the job six months after starting. If you can't execute, it's not a strategy.

- **Take your time**—Don't expect to get this right in one afternoon. I can take months arranging and rearranging a strategy until all the elements are present and it makes sense. You have to research, make phone calls, take meetings and build a really solid foundation of basic understanding. It actually takes longer to make a strategy simple than it does to make it long and convoluted.

There needs to be a counterpoint to strategy, and it is this: the strategy serves the goal. The strategy is not the main game. I say this because many people new to business perhaps become too focused on being prepared and having a plan, and they hold on to the plan harder than they hold on to the goal. Let me give you an example. A couple of years before the GFC struck Australia, my property development company built a block of apartments in Vaucluse, in Sydney's Eastern Suburbs. The apartments went on sale right as the panic hit financial markets, and the price that we'd planned to be paid for these very nice units could not be achieved. We were being offered 20 per cent less for each apartment than we'd budgeted for, and given that the profit margin on property developments is 30 per cent, it was not looking good.

So what should you do? If I was a younger person, I perhaps would have held on and tried to fight through, keep the apartments, lease them, refinance them, sell them a year later. And this is what many first-time developers would do. Me? I took what the market would bear and closed out that project. Why? Because the goal was to make a 30 per cent profit. When the goal became impossible to achieve, there was no point simply holding onto the strategy. The strategy always serves the goal. The goal is not to implement the strategy, regardless of the objective conditions.

DISCIPLINE

So you have a goal and you have a strategy. Now you have to execute. People who work with me probably think I use the word 'execute' too much. But for me, once you've settled on a goal and strategy for getting there, the action has to start. And the action has to be resolute, relentless and imbued with self-belief. In this respect, I use the word 'discipline' to describe the overall context: the ability to overcome fear and misgivings and *execute* according to your goals and strategy.

The execution is the hundreds of actions you perform every day to make your planning a reality. It takes discipline to do this, as well as lots of energy, intelligence, focus and self-belief. But at the heart of the person who can plan a venture, and then execute it, is discipline. Many business plans have stumbled on this, as have many plans to enter a new job or corporation and work towards a career goal.

In my lifetime, discipline has shifted from being a basic element of a successful personality, to being something to be sneered at and ridiculed. However, in the world in which I operate, discipline is still honoured and it is rewarded. Now more than ever, those who can show it are able to move up the corporate ladder faster than others; and people who can show discipline in their own businesses are always better equipped than their ill-disciplined rivals.

Discipline is a tool and it's a tool that makes the goal and strategy relevant. Here's what I think it takes to become disciplined:

- **Flexibility**—Being disciplined in following your goal and strategy does not mean having rocks in your head. Anyone with ambition to start a successful business or reach the heights in a corporation needs to be flexible enough to change the plan when circumstances dictate. Good discipline is not just the ability to keep going, it is also the ability to call a halt and reassess the success of what you're doing.

- **Listening and looking**—One of the reasons I prefer terms such as 'discipline' and 'execution' to describe this phase is because many first-time business people think that they have to be closed to the world and so single-minded that no competing ideas can get in. But in the business world—especially at start-up—you have to have a really good balance between strong focus on your goals and plan, and an openness to the market in which you operate. Discipline, for me, includes not only that strongly focused feeling I get when I'm chasing a goal, but an ability to hear and see everything. The market is a dynamic, changing, loud and colourful place. If you're going to understand it and anticipate it, you must be listening and looking. This is particularly the case for ambitious people in employment: yes, you have to stay focused on your goals and strategy, but your execution has to account for the dynamic realities in which you operate. Which brings me to some important concepts.

- **Tactics**—If strategy is the line that connects you to your goal, tactics are the many small adaptations you make during execution, to keep you on that line. Strategy is about planning—tactics are about execution. Often in businesses built on partnerships, you have the 'vision guy' and you have the person who 'makes it happen'. This really means the difference between a strategist and a tactician. Most business owners will have to be both, and just because you are making tactical changes doesn't mean the strategy is shot. Let's say the strategy was to attain a high standard of coffee by installing certain coffee-making machines in your café and using a quality brand of coffee bean. If you have to change your bean supplier and you install different machines to the ones envisaged, you can still be on track with the strategy of having a high standard of coffee. You just made a tactical adjustment—the strategy remains. Don't be afraid to make these tactical decisions during the execution phase. Stay focused on what's important.

- **Dealing with fear**—One of the biggest disrupters to otherwise well-qualified entrepreneurs is the fear of failing. For many people, discipline is the only thing standing between success and a total loss of confidence. You must work on this part of yourself if you want to take on audacious ventures. It isn't about having no fear. Anyone who does something worthwhile will have fear and doubt. It's about having enough self-discipline to keep going, to stick to the plan, and not be spooked. I have enjoyed enough success, in a high profile way, that people assume I have nothing to be scared of. But I feel fear on a weekly basis. I get myself into situations where failure is not an option and I become as nervous about financial ups and downs as anyone. My current business, Yellow Brick Road, was started in 2007 with my own money. I remember sitting in a hotel room in Athens in 2008 as Wall Street melted down and I watched BBC, CNN and Sky for 24 hours, trying to make sense of the magnitude. Yes, I'd set up a financial services firm right on the eve of the GFC. Fear was a constant for me from 2008 through to the end of 2009, as liquidity dried up and financial markets rolled back like a tide. It was a very frightening time but I had to keep going. There are several ways of dealing with fear that work for me. Firstly, I don't deny fear—I acknowledge it and have a strategy for it. Secondly, I make myself see fear in the context of the good things, the positives that are arising out of what I'm doing. And thirdly, I ensure I do daily exercise in order to keep my body healthy and my mind fresh. In particular, I do yoga, not just for its meditative qualities, but because it makes you breathe. Here's a hint for those who feel fear and have to work through it: one of the first things affected when you're scared is your breathing. You either hyperventilate or you hold your breath. Yoga makes you breathe properly.

- **Watch your money**—Many first-time business owners will sluice through their cash in the first few months of opening simply because they have never had to deal with suppliers and trade terms before. This is when you need discipline: you have to stick with the cash flow projections and stay within budget. And if you can't do that yourself, you have to bring in a finance person who can do it for you.
- **Learn from mistakes**—We meet people, we make alliances and we make decisions based on these interactions. Sometimes

they are the wrong decisions. It is a natural part of the business world that at some point a person who knows more than you can take advantage of that fact and hurt you and your business. When I was in my late twenties and I owned a professional services firm, I was keen to get into property developing. I was approached by a very successful person who drove a Rolls Royce, was a member of the Lakes Golf Club and seemed to have all the trappings of a successful man. He was quite a bit older than me, as were the four other investors he'd collected as a property syndicate. The idea was to pitch in with cash, buy one property in Kings Cross and then borrow to buy the building next door. I put in my money and we got a mortgage for the other property. About six months later, when we were looking at designs for the new development, I had a call from a liquidator: he knew I was part of the syndicate and he told me that there'd been no payments made on the mortgage and the bank wanted the property sold. My payments had been sent to the leader of the syndicate, the guy in the Rolls Royce, who had loaded everything into a couple of containers—including the car—and taken off for Taiwan. It was my first property development deal and I'd been taken. The lesson? Don't let flattery blind you. As it happened, I fought with the others in the syndicate to keep the property, and we sold it and closed out the mortgage. We all lost six months worth of mortgage payments and it was a very embarrassing deal; but it taught me that if you have a mentally disciplined approach, you'll be able to bounce back or correct your course much more easily than those who are wishy-washy about what they're doing.

Discipline does not stop mistakes, but it gives you a better chance of bouncing back.

- **Tell yourself it's worth it**—Discipline and adherence to the plan is an important self-reinforcement technique. It is you telling yourself that the plan works and you deserve the success that comes from it. Failing to do this means you are really failing yourself.

There are many ways to achieve this—a three-stage way is what works for me and for many people. As a personal aside I would remind people that a certain amount of flexibility is always worth building into your plans. Since I founded Yellow Brick Road in 2007, the goal has altered slightly, as has the strategy. My early approach to building lots of branches didn't include having partners such as Channel Nine and Macquarie Bank, but the conditions changed post-GFC and both of my new partners had their reasons to want to be invested in a growing financial services company, and I saw good reason to make those partnerships. While I like planning and I trust the adherence to your goals, you also have to acknowledge that you operate in a dynamic market in which things are always changing, and you are also operating in cycles—regular ups as well as downs. So even though I have a reputation as being tenacious about goals and strategies, I always keep flexibility in my back pocket. However, when I say flexibility, I don't mean giving yourself an easy way out when thing get tough. Flexibility for me is a way to take advantage of the inevitable changes that are occurring in your market.

CHAPTER 6

SO YOU WANT YOUR OWN BUSINESS

In the modern economy senior employees and business owners face many of the same challenges: hiring, building teams, working towards goals, showing leadership, staying inside budgets, returning value to shareholders, developing strategy and delivering on promises. They are aspects shared by both. However, there are some challenges that apply to business owners alone and I want to specifically deal with these.

BEFORE YOU JUMP IN

How you approach building your own business will always be slightly different to how you operate as an employee. Not better, not worse, but certainly different. For a start, business owners carry the fortunes of the enterprise on their own shoulders. Even when they install managers and executives to run the firm—or parts of it—the owner still feels that responsibility. It never goes away.

Then there's the question of remuneration. Business owners often pay themselves less than the senior employees, and grant themselves a dividend if things are going well. But an employee is free to go where the salaries are the biggest. It's the same for entitlements: employees have sick days, paid leave and superannuation. Business owners make their own arrangements.

If an employee makes a big mistake—or does something negligent or criminal—the business owner pays for this as if it's their mistake. And business owners always stake their own capital in their ventures, even when they take on partners and borrow from the banks.

So business owners are always on the clock. It takes over their lives. This will always be the differentiator between business owners and employees, regardless of how hard employees work and how much responsibility they take on. And when this is all factored in, the business owner takes risk: the risk they can lose it all.

So here's a basic challenge for those who want to buy or start a business: it will take over your entire life. Is this really what you want to do? Have you investigated life as a business owner, or are you fantasising about the grass being greener?

GETTING TO KNOW YOURSELF

There are so many different types of businesses and business scenarios that it's not always helpful to look at a random business and see how you'd fit in. I think it's smarter for those wanting to start a business to begin with a simple audit of themselves and whether they are suited for a life of business ownership. I'm not talking about personality typing, of the kind that recruitment companies and corporations routinely do. There are many different personality types in the ranks of business owners, just as there are many different business types: there is a person suited to running the suburban solicitor firm and there is someone suited to running a tech start-up. I'm talking about aligning your true self with your business aims, the extent to which you can handle the grinding and stressful nature of running a business, and the basic issue of whether your talents and abilities are good enough that customers will pay for them.

These three aspects may seem quite separated, or at best loosely connected. One is an idealistic height to be aimed for; the second is an acceptance of the practical exigencies such as balancing revenues with outgoings, provisioning for tax and paying employees; and the last one concerns your talent, which can be developed and honed.

Yet, they are equally important in the end because a weakness in one or two of these areas is going to make for an unhappy business life. I know of business owners who are doing their life's work, but they feel they are drowning in red tape and financial demands. I know other business owners who like the challenge of getting their financial controls and revenue models in order, yet they lament that they didn't have the guts or foresight to start a business that reflects their passion. And then there are people out there with tonnes of talent, but no business sense and no feeling that they are doing what is really in their heart.

The optimum, of course, is to own a business which reflects

your purpose, allows you to showcase your talents and where the administrative burden is not too great. But what of the other extreme? What about feeling crushed by the pressures of money, regulation and taxes, and also being quite divorced from your purpose and not using your talents? This is a bad situation to be in and as with most remedies for business problems, it starts early and it starts with you.

You don't think about the bad times when you're making your business plans, developing your product and producing your business cards and brochures. And you don't think about the yoyo journey of revenues when you're producing spreadsheet budgets. But ask anyone who's owned a business for a while and they'll tell you that even a good week will throw up unexpected events and nasty surprises, and that when all the employees and advisers have gone home, it's just you sitting there trying to work out how to get through without fear and stress overcoming you. And it's in these nervous and lonely times that you'll need to know that you have what it takes—that you are actually doing what you should be doing, that it's all worth it, that it counts for something.

So before putting all your money into a business, think about who you are, your strengths and weaknesses, and what it is that you bring to the enterprise and the industry it operates in. A bit of self-knowledge at the beginning might save you many missteps later in the process.

WHAT'S YOUR PURPOSE?

I've alluded to this earlier in the book. Purpose is easy to sneer at, easy to question as being undefinable. It's the kind of thing that many business 'experts' try to steer clear of. Either they can't fit it into their spreadsheets and their models for business success; or they don't see why it's necessary; or they don't want their clients talking about their purpose because this would take the discussion outside of the consultant's purview.

This is, therefore, one of those areas in which the prospective or current business owner has to assume their own leadership. You're really on your own with this. Yet it's very important in my opinion, because one of the great certainties of all business is that you will have tough times along with the good, and when those tough times hit, you'll need an anchor: you'll need to know that you're doing what you should be doing, that you're fulfilling your purpose.

One of the mechanisms I have for dealing with stress and fatigue is based on purpose. Once a week I like to wander over to the Botanic Gardens in Sydney and let the sun touch my face, feel the breeze and think about why I'm working so hard. It's my trigger for reminding myself that my purpose is to assist people to own a home and to help them retire in comfort. These fundamentals are important to me and I want to provide them to others. It's my purpose.

There's a number of ways to find your purpose. The easiest is the purpose that has always been with you. If you've had a lifelong desire to be an architect, builder or gardener, then becoming qualified and experienced and going into business for yourself are natural steps to take. It has been a clear journey.

But not everyone has this clarity of purpose in their lives. In fact, most of us don't. For these people—who are employed at someone else's business or are trying to break out of a business rut they are already in—the best way to begin your investigation is to concentrate on the 'why' in your life, and separate it from the 'what' or the 'who'.

How does this work? Well, if someone asks you about your purpose, and you say, 'To reach my goals', then you're not talking about purpose. Your goal is a 'what', not a 'why'. Some people—when I ask them about purpose—will say, 'To support my family'. But that isn't really a purpose, either: that's a 'who', not a 'why'. They're really saying, 'These are the people who rely on me'.

Your purpose is not a reason or an excuse or a goal. Your purpose should answer the question, 'Why?' In this regard, your purpose can be selfish and narcissistic. It isn't really about anyone else, it's about you; it isn't external, it's internal; it isn't objective, it's personal. Your purpose should come from your soul, not your brain, and it's therefore likely to be a self-serving and self-satisfying answer.

FINDING YOUR PURPOSE

Let's say you want to start a real estate firm. You might have goals and benchmarks, and you will have a business plan which sets out your strategy, your market and what sort of sales you need to reach your goals. But purpose is more personal. When you ask, 'Why do I want to own this firm?', your answer could be phrased as, 'Because it's important to help people find a good place to live.' Or it could be, 'Because my home is important to me and I want to give people my expertise in finding their own home.' So not only does purpose go to answering 'Why am I doing this?' but it also gets to the essence of you.

If you want to start a business or you're trying to revamp the one you own, and you're floundering around a bit, it could be because you're not articulating your purpose properly. You can do this in two ways. The first is to begin with a list of what describes your essence, and construct a business case from that. The second is to start with finding the essence of the business and seeing if this fits with your 'why'.

When you're working with a list, simpler is better: try listing every situation that makes you feel happy. It doesn't have to be a list that impresses fellow workers on a corporate retreat. There are no prizes for being deep or sensitive, not when it's your own business and your own money on the line. Let's say your 'happiest' list looks like this:

1. When I'm playing golf.
2. When I'm watching a movie with my kids.
3. During my first coffee of the day.

There is nothing wrong with divining the essence of yourself from such a basic list. Personally, I trust simple motivations more than complicated ones. From the above list, you could look at it and admit to yourself that your essence involves something physical (golf), something emotional (family) and something sensual (that first coffee).

You don't need to immediately create a business plan around one or all of these things. What you're doing is creating an honest conversation with yourself which can turn into an appraisal of your essential self. And your essential self always knows when it's happy—that's why you have to start by listing what has made you happiest.

With the above list, you can be happy when you're around coffee or by providing golf equipment or experiences. Perhaps you can even develop a business around that feeling you have with your kids. If nothing else, putting yourself through this process forces you to think about what matters to you, what's in your heart.

The second way of clearly articulating your purpose is to define the essence of your business—or the business you want to start or buy—and focus on whether this touches any personal nerves. In the above examples, we could say that if you own a café the essence of that business is providing a beautiful warm drink in a relaxed safe atmosphere, first thing in the morning. Does this strike a chord with you? Yes, it does, because you're at your happiest when having that first coffee of the day—you know how important it is. Or perhaps you're thinking of buying a golf shop. One of the things that makes you happiest is playing golf, and so you think to yourself there's a good fit there.

When establishing your purpose, however, I'd look beyond the obvious connections: just because you like playing golf doesn't mean you'll like being a retailer. The essence of a golf shop is providing golf equipment to those who love playing golf. If you own a shop, you're providing goods to customers. You're not necessarily playing golf. The essence of the golf shop is providing, not playing. Perhaps you need to go deeper into the essence of your love for golf? Perhaps you like using your body in such a way that you execute the perfect shot? Maybe that gets you close to the truth about yourself.

•

In the end, purpose is one of those personal journeys and few people get it right the first time they try to define it for themselves. Basically, purpose is that feeling you get when you're doing precisely what it is that you should be doing. Some people are lucky; it comes to them when they're young and it's a 'calling'. Sports stars and musicians tend to hear this calling at a young age. Most of us have to work at it, establish what it is and then define it. But it's worth the effort—it's something that will keep you going when there are so many reasons to give up.

CHAPTER 7

THE REALITY OF BUSINESS OWNERSHIP

You have to know what you're doing if you want to form a business around it. If you start an IT consulting business, you should know about computers; if you buy a hair salon, you should know how to cut hair. Because of this competence premium, pre-existing ability is certainly one of the most common ways to enter the business world—to take what you know or what you're good at and sell it in the market. This can happen in obvious ways and also in ways that are tangential and need a little thinking.

TALENT AND EXPERTISE

Expertise can make a big difference to how a business develops. Essentially, expertise means having knowledge or experience that is very rare or even not available to your rivals—let's call it 'talent'. You need to add hard work, luck and persistence, but if you have talent in the right place and in the right amount, you have a clear advantage over your rivals.

I use the word 'talent' broadly, because I don't limit it to someone who's a professional tennis player or a violinist in an orchestra or a renowned painter. This is innate talent. Another kind of talent is an attitude or a knowledge you've been imbued with because you've been raised in an environment that's involved in an industry: horse-racing families, diamond merchant families and construction families all spin-off second and third generation experts because they've been raised understanding something from the inside that seems impenetrably difficult from the outside.

Then there's the talent that most people have: acquired talent. By this I mean the person who's curious, smart and hard-working who goes into an industry or profession and develops a talent by sheer application and will. I consider that after three years of hard work and focus, you probably have talent at what you do. Some call this the '10 000 hour rule'.

WHAT'S YOUR TALENT?

When you look at some of the greatest people or organisations in history, you notice these four things: hard work, timing, risk, talent.

I will get to the others later but let's concentrate on the talent. You can be taught hard work, you can be lucky with timing and risk-taking is a relative formula (what might seem risky for a suburban lawyer is simply interesting for Richard Branson). But talent can't be fudged.

Think about Google, Microsoft, Bell Telephone, General Electric and News Ltd. All of these organisations were built by people who had a talent: Larry Page and Sergey Brin were PhD candidates at Stanford University, whose research project into page-links on the World Wide Web turned into an algorithm around which the Google search engine is based; Microsoft was built by Bill Gates and Paul Allen, who realised the need for user-interface software for computers and set about making the systems that now dominate the personal computer industry; Bell Telephone was founded by Alexander Graham Bell, who developed the telephone in the 1870s with Thomas Watson, while they were supposed to be inventing something else; General Electric was formed by Thomas Edison, who invented and developed things such as the light bulb, electrical power transmission along wires and the industrial fan; Rupert Murdoch took his father's one-newspaper company and expanded it into a global media and entertainment giant.

They all had help and luck and shifting markets happened to be ready for what they could offer. But they had one thing in common—not only did they have a talent, they knew what it was.

Many people do not accurately know what their talent is. They are smart, educated, experienced and have CVs that look perfect. But when I interview them or work with them, I see a quality coming out that is actually more coveted than the marketing material that pads out their résumé.

So I would start by advising people who are building a business, or who want a new start in their career, to go back to the beginning and ask: What am I bringing to the table?

LOOK AT YOUR SKILLS

From my perspective, I think talent should be thought about from both ends: not simply, 'What can I do?' but also, 'What am I really capable of?'

If you are a qualified engineer or a doctor—especially one with a speciality—you have credentials, degrees and other pieces of paper that say you have the talent and knowledge to perform certain tasks. This is a crucial question to start with: do I have the ability, the knowledge and the experience to sell my goods and services to the market? Some people have the pieces of paper. Others may have to get the pieces of paper before they start their business. And others will have to collect examples of their work, a folio of pictures, a website stacked with their efforts, etc. However it works, having the capacity to supply the service or product is a crucial beginning to starting a business. If you have lousy aim, don't be a house painter.

While these are straightforward examples of linking an ability with your business, there are less obvious paths. You may have worked at a business and developed a certain niche ability, and you're now deciding if you can build a business around that talent. This is actually a good way to form a business if you do your market research and get it right. In the 1990s, when mortgage brokers were becoming more common as a way to get a home loan, a lot of loan managers from banks and building societies were leaving their employers and setting up their own mortgage broker firms. You see the same thing when government departments from time to time offer their managers voluntary redundancy. The skilled people take the pay-out and set up their own consulting firms, because they have developed knowledge and insights that can be sold as services.

Most businesses that you can think of are formed in this way: a person—or a partnership of people—with common or complimentary skills set up a firm to sell those skills. Accountants, engineers, mechanics, removalists, truck drivers, private detectives, etc. The business is driven by what the owner is good at.

While this linear approach works for many business owners, it leaves some feeling a bit flat after a few years. Part of the problem for these people is the situation I canvassed above: the lack of clear purpose. They are performing a capability rather than pursuing a purpose.

For this reason, I believe there's other ways of thinking about talent that doesn't simply send you into a career tunnel that never lets you out and doesn't allow you to connect with what really matters. One option is to break down your skills or professional abilities into component pieces and ask of each component: 'How can this be developed?', 'Where can I take this?', 'What could this ability become?', 'Is there a market for this?'

Let's say you're a lawyer in a mid-sized firm and you've been thinking about starting your own business based on conveyancing. You can open a law firm specialising in conveyancing, with another lawyer who has skills in estate planning or business structuring. Or, you can break down your abilities and be clearer about what it is you actually do. Perhaps your list would look like this: good at dealing with upset people; good written communicator; excellent at negotiating with large companies; good at prosecuting arguments, getting results. And so on.

You may have the attributes to be something other than a lawyer—you could be a movie producer or a property developer or a mining consultant. This is where an appraisal of your actual abilities—not just your last job description—might take you.

Or you can try this. Break down your current legal career into a list of the clients that made you feel the most fulfilled. Think of the client who made you think, 'Gee, I wish I could do this every day.' The skills you used for that client are the skills you should think about when assessing your talent and how it could be developed, and where it could be used in your own business. In all likelihood, the client work that made you happy is precisely what you should be building your new business around. It doesn't matter if you only did that kind of work once or twice, and you don't think of yourself as an expert at it. Develop it as a serious part of you, talk about it as a core strength and see what you can do with it.

The same goes for knowledge. I am aware of some really interesting success stories from people who have known something very niche and formed their own business with the intention of making everyone who wants that niche service come to them. Michael Bloomberg, the Mayor of New York City, started a service for Wall Street bond traders which simply showed the prices being paid for treasury bonds at every bank on Wall Street. It was a very niche, very specific service for a narrow band of people. But he understood his market and they came to him for his knowledge. Today it's the Bloomberg media conglomerate, but it started with a tiny piece of knowledge.

Anyone in any job has a specific knowledge of something that most people don't. Sometimes, when we're in these jobs, we're too close to the action and we lose sight of what might be interesting or valuable to a potential market. While you're still at your job, and before you leap into your own business, I suggest you start listing what it is you do, what it is you know, and the kind of things you do each week to solve problems and shift roadblocks for either your employer or their customers. These problem-solving actions or processes—which you take for granted—are valuable to someone. Could you make a business out of them? Is there a technology that would help you do this? Are there people you would need to employ in order to do it? Are there customers for these services? Is anyone else doing it?

By looking at what makes you tick in the talent department—rather than simply which job you've had for the last five years—you give yourself a much broader idea of what is going to interest you in business. And what is likely to be successful for you, too, since you are more likely to be acting positively and confidently in a business you are excited about than one you just fell into.

It is true that you are unlikely to make much in way of revenues if you are not good at what you do. Every business needs competence at its heart. But simply opening a business because that's what you do—or because that's who you think you are—may ultimately feel uninspired.

There is another way to define your talent, and that is to start not with the thing that you see, but the part you should be seeing. Most people know if they can do their job. But the next step with your talent is understanding what you really have of value. It's worth taking time with this before committing yourself to a business.

ARE YOU UP FOR IT?

Having assessed purpose and talent, let's get into the knitting and get you asking yourself: are you up for this? Many people either fail or drop out of business because they didn't really think about what they can and cannot handle in a working life.

Much of the work of being in business is not glamorous: it is stressful, difficult and unrewarding. Very few people will see you doing this basic leg-work, no one will pat you on the back for it and it is highly unlikely you will ever be paid what you're worth for it. It's the daily grind, and if you haven't done this before, here's a few starting questions that are particularly relevant to running a business:

- Can you rise at 5.30 a.m., work all day, get to bed late and get up the next day and do it all again?
- Can you operate under stress and fear?
- Do you love a challenge?
- Do you love hard work?
- Are you relentless, curious, adaptable and disciplined?
- Can you handle irregular income?
- Are you comfortable phoning a debtor to have an invoice paid?
- Can you motivate staff, drum up sales, deal with banks?

I don't like to discourage people from starting a business, because I find the effort of running an enterprise exhilarating and very satisfying. So who am I to turn someone away who really wants to give it a shot? However, I've had enough people approach me over the years, asking about going into business, to be highly aware of issues concerning personal compatibility. Some people simply are not equipped to deal with the constant stress and uncertainty of business ownership. This is not a judgement or insult: it's an observation based on a lot of experience, not only with business owners approaching me for advice and help, but also with those who have partnered with me as branch owner-managers first at Wizard Home Loans and then Yellow Brick Road. Over the years I've had to develop a system for ensuring that the right people are buying and managing these branches. And I've learned to start with the individual, because if you don't have the right person running a business, both the customers and the business owner suffers. No one is happy.

So, as you appraise yourself for life in business, get this part right. Don't fool yourself about a life of freedom or doing your own thing. If you want to know if you're up for this, here are a few things to think about:

- **Have you got the money?**—The majority of businesses take at least two years before the revenues reach a point where most of the start-up debt and costs are paid and they are into 'cash flow positive' territory. Add to that the effort to get sales to a certain point and you can expect two years of lean living, long hours and hard work. After that, income can be lumpy depending on how the business is travelling.
- **Red tape**—There's a good reason why every federal opposition promises to cut red tape for business owners, and that's because it is the one thing that all owners complain about. There is a mountain of regulation to sort through in many business sectors and you will not be paid for staying current with the regulations and applying for all your licences and permits. It adds to stress.

- **The burden of tax**—Your business may have its ups and downs but you never stop paying taxes and you never stop worrying that you got it right. Unlike being an employee—where the employer does your taxes for you—the business owner carries 100 per cent of the burden for getting their taxes right, every time. If you get it wrong, you might be prosecuted. But more likely the Australian Tax Office will accept your mistake, issue an assessment and give you a month to pay the arrears. Not everyone wants to carry this burden.

- **Can you handle employees?**—Even the best employees will not have the same enthusiasm towards your business as you do. This is the burden of proprietorship and it is the same for the smallest business or the biggest. Employees come and go and they all need to be managed. If you hire a good bunch, consider yourself lucky. Most business owners have at least one employee-related problem a week that they have to deal with. Who else is going to do it?

- **Are you a leader?**—If you want the best out of your employees, you'll have to lead. You don't get to outsource that role, and there are times when it is tiring. If you can't show leadership on a constant basis, you might like to rethink being a business owner. As a business gets bigger, you can install managers. But in most businesses the owner is the leader and it's a 24/7 job.

- **Time management**—When you work for an employer, time is a different commodity to when you work for yourself. You may think you're punctual and conscientious when you're an employee, but when you're a business owner, time—as they say—is money. One of the great challenges for people leaving the corporate world and starting their own business is time management. From running your own diary, to prioritising where you spend your hours, to managing where your employees spend their hours, time management will be a constant feature of being a business owner. Accept this before starting.

- **Your family**—The business owner is not the only one becoming tired and stressed with the job of starting an enterprise. Their family also gets caught up in the dramas and financial issues associated with the business. When sales are good, this is a good time for the family. When business is not so good, the whole family suffers with you. There are tricks you can use to get around this, which I will raise later. But those new to business should understand this: the family is usually a part of it.

This is a basic audit of yourself—a starting point to get you thinking about owning a business and what you can bring to it. As I say, keep it simple: make sure you have a purpose, a talent and an idea of what business owners actually do. If you have concerns about some or all of these criteria, slow things down a bit and think it through.

CHAPTER 8

WHAT SORT OF BUSINESS OWNER ARE YOU?

Let's assume you feel up to the task of starting a business. Then you get into what kind of business you should be pursuing. Again, this decision should be taken from the perspective of who *you* are. Know what your business motivations and dreams are and the rest starts to fall into place.

TO WORK OR TO GROW

There are, broadly speaking, two types of people in business, and these people fit within fairly clear guidelines. The two types I'm talking about are focused on one of two things, but usually not both:

- job
- growth.

This is not a competition or a judgement. I know both types and get along with them equally well. However, everyone who opens a business does so with different goals and values, and I believe that establishing which category you broadly fit into is an important step to go through before setting your own criteria. Doing so helps you define your goals, assists with knowing what is important and is crucial in understanding whether you're prepared to give what it takes. It decides what type of ventures you should commit. And, if you're on the lookout for a partner or key employees, it delineates the kind of people you can work with, and those you can't.

A growth-oriented business owner will not be happy if they mistakenly commit to a franchise with a strict business system implemented and enforced by someone else; and a person who thought they were buying a job but finds themselves dealing with Silicon Valley types and venture capitalists may simply want to run a mile. Some people are excited and energised by the challenge of growth. Others want a regular pay cheque for their efforts and are scared by uncertainty.

So it's worth knowing which one you are before committing to your venture. It might save you a lot of heartache and restlessness later on.

JOB-FOCUSED

If you are job-focused, you're typically interested in:

- low risk
- regular cash flow

- security of position
- predictable hours
- little or no volatility
- a mix of lifestyle criteria with business ambitions.

Job-focused people exist as business owners and employees. They operate at both the highest levels of the professions and in neighbourhood small business; they operate at low levels of a corporation and also at the head of multimillion dollar-turnover businesses. The job-oriented person is not defined by their circumstance as much as they are by their outlook.

In the employed sense, a job-focused person can be very competent, educated and even ambitious, in a certain way. Their focus is on securing a position that creates enough income to satisfy their need for food, shelter and social participation, and which gives them the chance to convert their revenues into a secure, slow-growing asset such as property. Job-focused employees work hard, do a good job and are usually loyal team-players who can drive a business towards success. But the key to their approach is this: the business they work for is an external part of their life. They see themselves as a 'taker'—a cost-centre—at their place of work, rather than a full participant. There's nothing wrong with that, except when you don't know that this is who you are. Job-focused people say, 'I work to live, not live to work,' and they are very comfortable with this. Or, should I say, they are comfortable with this outlook so long as they don't end up in a workplace where the leader wants them to contribute to the medium-term goals of the business.

The job-focused person also exists in the world of business owners. Many people who want to go into business are not risk-takers and are as adverse to volatility and uncertainty of income as their brothers and sisters in employment.

Generally, the job-oriented business owner looks to buy a business that already has a trading record and full books. There are accountants and solicitors who help these business owners to buy the lowest-risk, highest-certainty enterprise. This often means a business that's a proven franchise, or established in a busy mall or shopping centre, or a business where you 'buy' income streams by buying a client list, or 'buy' a job by buying a business with solid net profit margin.

In most industries, the price of a business is determined by a multiple of gross earnings. Let's say, for instance, that someone wants to buy an established café in a mall: the business will be valued at 2 × annual earnings. If the annual revenues are $150 000, then the business can be yours for $300 000.

In paying the $300 000, the job-focused business owner is essentially buying herself a job. The earnings are clear and predictable, the overheads are predictable, and the situation—a position in a mall with a certain amount of passing foot traffic—is established. The only ingredient missing is the new owner stepping in and adding their labour. They usually work in the business and employ a couple of people, often family members.

There is nothing wrong with owning a business for these reasons as long as you understand what it is you're doing. The money you take home each week—after the rent, supplies, taxes, business purchase loan repayments and wages—is really your salary. You have bought yourself a job.

GROWTH-FOCUSED

If you are growth-focused, you are typically interested in:

- higher risk
- capital gains
- proprietorial
- long hours
- volatility in order to attain goals
- a devotion to business.

Growth-focused people can be business owners or employees. Their essential difference to their job-focused counterparts is how they see the world. To the growth-driven person, a business is an entity that must grow, whether it be by increasing sales, profit, employees, branches or market share. In this respect, growth-oriented people see inherent value in a business rather than the business as something that simply pays them.

In practical terms, the person who buys a job when they buy a business is looking to take cash flow out of the entity on a weekly or fortnightly basis, whereas the business grower has their eye more focused on what the entire business will be worth in, say, three years time. So if a job-focused person buys a café for $300 000 because it will give them an income of $150 000, the business grower thinks about it the other way around: 'If I add features and improve this business, I can sell it for $500 000 in three years.' Or they might think about it in the following terms: 'If I can lift the annual revenue to $250 000, then I can buy another café and use the same improvement techniques there that I learned here.'

It doesn't matter if you want to build an empire or build a business so you can sell it for a capital gain, it's the mentality that's crucial: the growth-focused owner always sees the future market value in a growing business rather than the immediate income from a static model.

This outlook is not confined to business owners, because there are also employees who are driven by the excitement and challenge of growth rather than a salary. Most people who are employed in the financial services industry are—to a certain extent—remunerated by their contribution to revenues growth. Most participants in Silicon Valley are prepared to forgo a large salary in order to focus on growing a business amidst obstacles that can revalue the business and, therefore, revalue their equity in it.

•

Many people who set out to become business owners make themselves miserable because they weren't honest about their own comfort level when they set out. Some businesses might be cheap to buy but they require work to get them to a point where they spin off the sort of set-and-forget income that a job-focused business owner wants. This might entail some marketing, rebranding, new goods and services, and some aggressive pricing. Look at an example of the neighbourhood florist shop. You might be on the lookout for a business that creates a job, but you buy a business in need of rebuilding and discover—too late—that you are not suited for that kind of entrepreneurial business life. This basic mismatch between personality and business is what makes people depressed and drives them out.

It also happens the other way around. A growth-minded person may start a phone shop from scratch only to discover that there is a natural ceiling to the growth in that business, in that location. The phone shop turns into a job and the growth-oriented owner loses interest.

As it happens, the market eventually sorts out these situations: the person who wanted to buy a job will buy the phone shop that's been built to a solid revenues platform by the business grower; and the growth-oriented business owner will buy the florist shop that needs work to take it to a new level.

The problem doesn't lie in being one of these people or the other—the problem lies in not knowing which one you are until you're committed to the wrong business. This is a common occurrence in the employment ranks, but less is at stake: you can bide your time, send out your CV, apply for other positions while still earning income. But when buying a business, your whole life savings might be plunged into the purchase and by the time you find out that it's the wrong business for your personality, it's too late: the leases have been signed, your employees are on-deck, and you have already borrowed money and made your capital purchases.

WHAT ABOUT YOUR EMPLOYEES?

Many readers will be landed with the situation where they are one type of person, but they are reliant on the other kind. This happens all the time in business, whether you own the business and are employing people, or you're a team leader in an employed set-up. Either way, you will have to wrestle with this conflict at least once in your life.

In my own experience, I have come to accept that not everyone I employ is going to have the same drive to grow a business as I have. The best I can hope for is that the key positions I fill will be people of a like mind, and that other positions probably require a more steady approach and I will find the right people for those. By taking this approach I don't have to drift into the ego-driven areas of management and proprietorship, where the organisation's leader feels that everyone has to be a mirror-image of themselves. That isn't healthy for the business and it isn't helpful for the employees.

It also works the other way. I know that many business owners who buy a franchise are not particularly interested in the large-scale growth that interests someone like me. In fact, most franchise owners have limitations about what expansions they can undertake on a geographical and product basis. So a person who buys herself a job when she buys the franchise will not be looking for the type of person that I want to put into key positions. If she mistakenly employees a hard-charging employee she will constantly feel as if she's losing control and the arrangement will not work.

Having made this distinction, I think most workplaces benefit from having a blend of growth-oriented and job-focused people. Even fast-growing businesses need their corporate and administrative workings to be conducted by solid, hard-working people, just as the oldest banks and insurance companies still need their growth-oriented people to keep finding ways to grow the pie. There are also many shades of grey between these two poles.

Finally, when it comes to the difference between the job-centred and the growth-oriented person, it is a big mistake to try to change who and what they are. When you own a business or run a team within one, there will be times when a person slips through and ends up in a position that is wrong for them. In fact, there will be many times when this happens. Either they will appear a bit too cautious and clock-driven, and that will irritate you, or they will be sending you emails late at night and trying to pursue new ideas.

The first thing you can do when you're working with the 'wrong' business personality is to think about where you can place them so that their natural outlook is better served. Or, you can let them go. Those really are your choices. What you can't do is change them. If you have someone in your team who feels the biological urge to leave the workplace at 5.30 p.m. and not think about work until 9 a.m. the next day, then attempting to change this outlook will drive you mad. Likewise, if you want someone to just sit at their desk for eight hours a day, get the job done and not have any new ideas—against all their instincts—then your efforts to change them will create problems much broader than the dynamic between the two of you.

There's only one way to get the right balance in your workplace and to ensure that the people in the key positions are appropriately growth-oriented or job-centred and that is to start with what you know best—yourself.

Start with an honest appraisal of whether you are growth-oriented or job-centred, and most other decisions in your business will flow from there.

In my own business I poll my people every Friday night by sending out a group email with some basic questions about the week. In around 150 branches for YBR, I have managers who also part-own the branches in a hybrid franchise structure. These people are crucial to not just sales of financial products, but also for the customer interface. I can't be in 150 places at once, but it is my company and I am a growth-oriented, highly curious person who always wants to know what's going on and how I can improve it for the customers. Which means I need my managers to be like this too. I log the responses to my emails on the basis of response time, quality of response and amount of information. I ask myself: is this person engaging with me? Are they interested in the branch and the customer? Curious about what the deal flow looks like and how to improve it? This is how I sort out who's who and whether they have that growth gene or they're making themselves unavailable over the weekend. Sometime I can be in my office til eleven at night on a Friday, answering all the responses. But that's okay. I know who I am and what I want and, as the employer, it's my job to find out where my people fit in: growth-oriented, or job-focused.

CHAPTER 9

BUSINESS TYPES

Personality is a really important part of developing a business. Your personality and the personality of those you employ. Starting with understanding yourself is crucial. It helps you select the people who will help—rather than hinder—you. But businesses also have 'personality', in some respects, and it's worth giving thought to which one you want to be associated with.

When I do business seminars, the audience fall into three main groups and I'm going to assume readers are divided into these groups, too. They are:

1. Business owners who are looking to revamp their existing business or expand into a new business.
2. Employees who are about to start their own business.
3. Employees who want to own their own business, though they don't necessarily know the area they want to go into.

There are probably more than these, but these are the main categories of people I speak to and who ask me questions. Each of them brings different issues.

I think it's a good idea to know who you are, what you bring and what you want to take away. Do you want to create, or do you want to follow in an established business format? Do you want fast growth or do you want solid revenues? Are you interested in high risk/high reward, or low risk/low volatility?

These are valid questions that go to the heart of what sort of enterprise you should be involved in, and which ones you should avoid at all costs.

BUSINESS MODELS

People who have come from salaried employment before they start a business—and that is almost all of them—usually come from a background of specific and technical knowledge, which is great to get things rolling, but it often means they find it hard to stand back from the business itself and see a broader business ecology. And because they can't see it all at once, they often miss important parts of the puzzle and make mistakes about what business they're building, where they want to go and what can be made out of what they have.

In my experience, the most basic failing is to not recognise aggregate demand or to assign it an importance in business planning. How important is demand? Every developed country runs its economy on 'monetary policy', which is aimed at increasing or decreasing aggregate demand for goods and services by changing the price of money via interest rates. Interest rates are merely the tool. The desired effect is to alter demand, because demand controls all destinies in a market economy.

So when inspecting a business idea or concept, remember in the first place that you are entering a marketplace that has an aggregate demand for goods and services, and you are trying to match this demand with supply. There are efficient ways to match the supply of your goods and services to the demand. These ways are called business models, and having the right one for the right industry at the right time is an important component of business success. Business models underpin every enterprise and while they are not always obvious to the casual observer, understanding them is as important to a business owner as the difference between an internal combustion, diesel and jet turbine motor is important to a mechanic. At the major business schools, students spend much of their time attempting to identify business models. You should understand them too and learn how to identify them in every business you see. You will definitely put yourself in a better position to create a successful business model for your own business, or at least understand the dynamics that contribute to a lack of performance. Here are the main ones.

DISRUPTION

The disruptive business model is probably the peak of the business pyramid and is run by the type of business person that most people are thinking about when they say 'entrepreneur'. Disruption is a high-profile business model because it involves a newcomer disrupting an existing market, typically controlled by a few powerful incumbents. The disruptor usually faces push-back from not only much larger and wealthier incumbents, but also a high barrier to entry: that is, the costs of competing are so high that most new entrants cannot operate with enough scale to drive sales and they soon give up.

A good example of a successful disruptor would be Richard Branson attempting to start his Virgin airline in the face of the obstructive incumbents British Airways and a British establish-ment which didn't want him to start an airline. Closer to home, my first large business—Wizard Home Loans—was a disruptive business model, attempting to break into the Australian mortgage market which was dominated by four banks in the 1990s, and still is today. In the 1970s, a small start-up company in a Californian garage challenged the IT incumbents with a new technology called the 'personal computer'. The company was Apple and it eventually overtook IBM, Honeywell, Hewlett-Packard and Burroughs, and is today the most valuable stock on the New York Stock Exchange. It was a disruptive business model.

However, examples such as these are quite rare. The truth is that most disruptors have to bow out, never to be seen again. When you look at the incumbents of the industries I've listed above, you wonder how anyone could attract enough capital to seriously make inroads into their established markets, from a standing start. But business owners make it work when a few of the following requirements align:

- **Demand**—There must be existing demand and the aggregate of it must be sufficiently large that a new player can come into the market and create revenues early by gaining even a very small slice of the market.

- **Distinction**—While the demand must exist, what you bring to the market has to be sufficiently different to what the incumbents are offering that the customers are drawn to what you are selling. The distinctive feature that most consumers notice is price, but price alone is not usually enough. Henry Ford introduced the Model T in 1908, into a market in which cars were made for wealthy people. He sold cars that people could afford, he made them accessible through dealerships across the world and they were reliable. He used existing demand, but created a . . .

- **New market**—In bringing something distinctive to existing demand, the disruptor creates a new market. Henry Ford's cheap, accessible, reliable Model T created a new market for cars: all those people who were not rich.

- **Advantage**—Every successful disruptor has an advantage, whether it's technology, access to materials, lower costs or better staff. Henry Ford had a production line that could produce Model T's at a price that opened up an untapped market for private automobiles; Apple had the technology to put a computer—then the preserve of large corporations and governments—in private homes; Virgin had a brand and a marketing machine that changed the image of flying.

- **Drive**—All disruptive business models have a driven, perhaps obsessive business owner behind them. Markets that are 'owned' by incumbent oligopolies are not surrendered easily and most challengers are repelled in the end because they don't have the energy for a long fight.

- **Choice**—Be aware that all the successful disruptive business models I've seen assume that consumers have a choice to shift to the new entrant and are able to make that choice without too great a penalty. Aggressive entrepreneurs need to be careful with this crucial element in the business model, because if the consumers are limited in how they can behave—usually by restrictive governments or caveats in the consumer agreements—then the disruptor will have trouble gaining sales.

- **Technology**—Many disruptive businesses burst into a highly controlled market because of a new technology or product. Apple did this in the mobile phone industry: it had never built a mobile phone until it launched the iPhone in 2007, bringing the touch screen and 'apps' into common usage. It currently has 20 per cent of the global smart-phone market. Technology disruption is usually of the evolution variety: a smart phone evolved from a mobile phone which evolved from a cordless landline. But there is also revolutionary technology disruption, where the technology is so new that it *displaces* previous technology. An example would be roads being displaced by canals, which was displaced by railways, which was displaced by motor cars, which was displaced by air travel. The art of a disruptive business model is not simply the technology itself, but the uses it is put to. The steam engine was invented at the start of the 1700s for pumping water out of coalmines: it wasn't until George Stephenson repurposed the engine for a railway in the 1820s that the transport revolution really began.

I have created and led several disruptive businesses, and even though they have found success, nothing about them has ever been easy. When a large incumbent sees a threat to its cosy revenues and established market position, it reacts by trying to undercut your prices, complain to regulators with vexatious allegations, tries to buy you out or attempts to steer the market away from you. And often all of these. It's a fight, and not only if you take on the big end of town such as the banks, airlines and phone companies. Disruption doesn't always take place on a national or international scale. You could see a chance to start a trucking company in competition with two major incumbents in a large regional town, because you have access to cheap vehicles. Or you could tender for local government contracts that are usually shared around by three incumbent businesses, because you have a new technology not owned by your rivals. The trick to being a disruptor is being very clear that whatever the outcome, you will be in for a fight from larger businesses that do not want to lose their market position. It will take over your life for a period of time and business owners should understand this before committing to it. Once again—know yourself.

ME-TOO

The me-too business is probably the most obvious model in any business environment. They are the businesses that model themselves on an enterprise that is already operating, attempting to either meet untapped demand for the goods or services being sold, or challenging the incumbents for the existing market share.

Typically this is how a me-too business works. Let's say you want to start a florist shop in a certain town. There's already a florist in that town, but because this is a large town of 22 000 people, you figure that it can handle two florists and both of you will make money.

Or you are a star salesman at a real estate agency and you leave your employer to start your own real estate firm across the street. You know how much work there is in your suburb and you know who will join you as an employee or as a partner.

In both of these scenarios, you are not challenging existing business models or introducing anything new to your industry. Your florist shop or real estate agency will have a different logo and different premises, but you are selling what everyone else is selling, and pretty much doing it in the same way as everyone else.

The me-too business is a double-edged sword which comes with strengths and weaknesses. On the strengths side, because the me-too business follows established business formats and pricing structures which are understood well by consumers, not a lot of rethinking has to be done in order to quickly have a viable business up and running. In this sense, it doesn't matter that there are two or three of the same services being offered in the one town, because they usually help to grow the market. If there are three florists or real estate agents in a suburb, rather than just one of each, then local consumers are trained to keep their business in that area rather than drive somewhere else. Along with it being easy for the business owner and acceptable to the consumer, the me-too business also fits a template that suppliers can fit into their credit policies and which banks can also measure when they assess you for finance.

But there are also problems with me-too business. Because there are few things that owners change about how they run, the main focus becomes price and incumbency. The incumbent business will not want to give up its market position and will usually fight on price—offering special deals and locking people into contracts, etc.—making it hard for the me-too business to get momentum with its revenues. The me-too business can also become bogged down in broader industry troubles, which it can't break out of because it hasn't differentiated itself. It lives and dies on industry trends rather than being capable of adapting.

Differentiator

There is another kind of me-too business which I call the 'differentiator'. For example, this is the appliance retailer which markets itself by differentiating what it supplies. It may market itself on the basis that it will do a deal for customers who pay in cash. A mortgage lender may differentiate itself by providing a service visiting people in their home or workplace. A lawyer might market herself on the basis that you only pay her if she wins the case.

These are me-too businesses that have differentiated themselves so they stand out in a vanilla market. You can probably think of examples of these: they should stick in your mind because that is their marketing rationale. They offer recognisable goods and services in a recognisable format—which promise comfort of delivery to the consumer—but with a differentiating twist to gain attention and get customers.

These businesses are a blend of me-too and entrepreneurial in that the business owner is having to challenge the market's known formats. In doing so, they challenge consumers to make a choice, which is what all entrepreneurs do.

The downside of these differentiator businesses is that often they have to spend more on advertising than the businesses they are differentiating themselves from. They operate on being different, so they can never relax—they're constantly having to reinforce this image. The upside is that the business owner is committed to a more creative approach to business which gives greater scope when the economy has a downturn or troubles hit the industry. It also gives the owner more room to create a specialty which eventually takes the business out of the realms of the me-too.

Technical-Professional

Most towns have the technical-professional me-too businesses such as accountants, lawyers, dentists and doctors. These businesses operate to accepted dynamics and margins and offer their services in generic ways. There is nothing wrong with predictable business models and industry-standard offerings, just understand this before opening such a business. There is not a lot of room for difference.

Niche

There are lots of small niche businesses that most of us have never heard of because they fulfil a very specific task in a specific industry, with little need for advertising. They install and maintain fire-fighting equipment on oil rigs; they underwrite insurance policies for circuses and rodeos; they supply parts and maintenance for German potato-picking machinery. These niche businesses are always top-heavy with expertise and experience, and are less reliant on marketing or brand-building. They are known in the industries they service, and as long as the service is excellent and the price not too high, they have long-term clients and steady sales.

The problem with these business models, from the perspective of a new business owner wanting to enter, is that their incumbency is hard to challenge: the clients are limited and the services and products have to be of a certain standard rather than at a cut-price. Entering a niche market from a cold start is usually successful when you're working in that industry and build a network of prospective clients before starting your business, or if you start with a business in an associated industry and branch into the niche. It's not unusual for a first-time business owner to assume that because they know everything about a niche they can hang out their shingle and enjoy quick success. Be careful of this assumption. Just knowing about your industry is not always enough.

ENTREPRENEURIAL

The entrepreneur is one of the more misunderstood business owners in the marketplace. People have visions of entrepreneurs being young billionaires inventing internet stuff, but in reality an entrepreneur is a person who can arbitrage supply and demand, before the demand is fully realised or recognised by the market. The result is a service or product that feels very new yet also seems so obvious for the times. It's as if the entrepreneur provides the product or services precisely when the demand for it is awakening. An example is Janine Allis's Boost Juice, which took the idea of juice bars from the US in the early 2000s and turned it into a global franchising phenomenon. The good entrepreneur arbitrages their unique supply against latent demand. If they get it right, and catch the consumer's imagination at the right time, they ride a wave.

Of course, the story of Allis and Boost Juice is not usual. Most entrepreneurs do not have this type of success. Most entrepreneurs have to fail a couple of times before they succeed. This is one of the reasons that the vast majority of new business ventures are me-too businesses: they sit in the middle of the road and have a greater rate of success, but not usually the huge profits.

VULTURES

There is a subset of entrepreneurs who buy distressed businesses that have been run to insolvency, then rebuild them for sale. These entrepreneurs—sometimes called 'vultures'—are usually experts in their industry, are experienced business people and are conversant with the earnings multiples that are charged for certain businesses.

They start with the earnings they have to produce in the business so that they can demand the price they want when they sell it two years later. Let's say one of these people buys a distressed café for $50 000. They build it back up, advertise as being under new management, and when the earnings are in the right range they sell it for $200 000 to someone who wants a me-too business. The people who can make this work not only have expertise in the industry that the business operates in, but they understand what the market will pay for and where the demand is. They are the embodiment of the person who is growth-focused.

BUILD TO FLIP

Also focused on growth are people who actually build a business, component by component, in order to sell for a certain capital gain. As their starting point, these build-to-flip entrepreneurs have an earnings target, which—when reached—makes the business worth a certain multiple on the open market.

It's tempting for people new to business to think that this is an easy or fortuitous way to make good money: typically the entrepreneur who does this takes a salary from the business while working in it and can still sell it for its earnings multiple when the right offer comes in. So not only does the entrepreneur get back in wages what she puts in as capital, but she also walks away with a tidy capital gain. Let's say you invest $80 000 in starting a dry-cleaning shop, and you sell it for $300 000 two years later. The price operates on an earnings multiple (let's say, 2 × annual revenues). But the business owner has paid herself $80 000 a year to manage the shop, allowing a certain amount of the investment to be paid back anyway.

In the example above, inexperienced people see this as a perfect way to make good money. But it's not easy. You need capital to get started, you need industry insight, a strong idea of who (or what kind of person) will buy your revamped business, and at exactly what valuation. It has to be a tight business with solid systems, contracted suppliers, sales growth and a low wages bill; it has to be tight because it will usually be marketed through the accountant/solicitor networks to first-time business buyers who want a me-too business. And there's still a chance no one will buy it. The upside of this kind of business activity is that if you can't find a buyer, you can always take earnings out of the business as salary. However, the downside is that if you screw it up, can't get the earnings, can't get the earnings multiple you wanted and you have to sell it to one of the vultures, you're shit out of luck. Build-to-flip businesses are for the experienced, smart players and I advise you to stay away from this kind of endeavour until you really know what you're doing.

FRANCHISE

Vultures and build-to-flip entrepreneurs are perhaps not well-known outside of the business world, but we are well aware of them inside it. They are similar to the professional home renovators who buy a run-down dump, renovate it and sell it at a large profit. All businesses created by vultures and build-to-flips have certain systems and organisational characteristics so that people new to business can walk straight in and start running their new business. Same as a house buyer has nothing more to do when they buy from a professional renovator.

The franchised business takes this 'turnkey' concept and produces from it a business system that can be rolled out over a large geographic area, in a short time, with low risk to the new owners and an ongoing income stream for the franchisers. Is this something you could think about as a business owner? Let's take the franchise from both the perspective of the franchiser and the franchisee.

FRANCHISER

One of the benefits of becoming a franchiser is that you can expand your business and your brand over a large area without the investment of capital that it would take if you funded this yourself. As a franchiser, your advantage is that you can put your efforts into developing the brand, the product, the financial systems, the marketing and the training. You create a model—or a map—for the success of your own business and sell aspects of this expertise to people who want to own a me-too business. This is the good part: you can create one set of systems, one brand and one testing ground, but still have your business rolled out across Australia and the world, run by people who are willing to buy the right to operate under your banner and who still push back a percentage to you. You, in effect, become more of a business coach and support player, helping others to make money.

Highly successful businesses have expanded this way, including not only well-known American brands such as McDonald's, but Australian businesses like Boost Juice. My own businesses, Wizard and Yellow Brick Road, have been built on partial franchise models so that the branch managers are also owners. I believe that in both of those businesses it was the most efficient way to expand and assume a large sales footprint, while also ensuring that the branch and the head office in Sydney had aligned business goals. In both cases it took some work to develop systems, manuals and procedures—as well as training, centralised IT platforms and support modules—to ensure that all of the expertise held by my core team could be rolled out to the franchisees. After all, this is what they're paying for.

The downside of becoming a franchiser is that, regardless of the amount of time and effort you put in—and fees paid to franchising experts—there is no guarantee that prospective business owners will buy into your franchise. You also face the problem early in the piece that you have to accept a low price for the franchising fees because you are still untested as a medium-term proposition. Another downside for certain types of people is this: once you sell a franchise, you agree to support and train and troubleshoot that branch for the life of the agreement. You may not be patient enough for this. Go back to self-evaluation: supporting and empathising may not be your bag. You may fit more naturally into the role of the vulture or the build-to-flip person who prefers to build their business, take their profit from a sale and move on.

FRANCHISEE

I leave this description until last because becoming a franchisee is really the polar opposite of what we started with: the entrepreneurial disruptor. While the disruptor accepts high levels of risk and uncertainty in their ventures, the franchisee is de-risking the transaction in buying a proven brand and product, with systems that take uncertainty out of sales growth, overheads, employment and operating margins. Some franchised concepts are so well documented and systemised that, upon signing the documents and putting down your money, it is a straight haul through the franchiser's training, into the start-up phase and then into doing business, right down to grand-opening events and how to invite the neighbourhood. The better franchise systems are so well organised and professional that the major banks lend the franchisees most of the amount of the franchising fee, knowing that there will be solid revenues from the venture. This is obviously an attractive feature for people who are job-oriented, risk-averse and who need certainty of income.

Many people expect that because I am of the entrepreneurial-disruptor business type, I have no time for franchising. But, of course, I am a franchiser myself and I believe in the idea of using the responsibility and self-resourcefulness of an owner to work in an accepted brand and to a centralised system. Personally, I wouldn't buy a business like this, because I know myself and I know that I enjoy the creative side of business and I am excited by challenge and risk. But that's me. Others who have been in employment for a long time, and need some structure around them, really like the franchisee role and enjoy the training and mentoring they get from this business model.

When buying a franchise, beware of what you're buying. Some franchisers reserve the right to introduce competition to your town or suburb at a later date, which can irk a franchisee who has done all the hard work of building the brand in that area. Also, promised support is not always forthcoming and if you have bought a franchise because you need that corporate support, it is going to feel lonely when you can't get it. And lastly, for many people who use their redundancy pay-outs—or other corporate severance payments—to buy a franchise, their dream is of the freedom of being a business owner. It's a dream of working for themselves. If this is the dream and the priority, be careful of how your franchiser runs the system. Some systems are incredibly strict about what you can and can't do, and will virtually spy on you to ensure compliance. For many people this may feel like being employed all over again, and the dream of being a business owner starts to disappear.

•

So there's a spectrum of business models, ranging from the entrepreneurial to the security-conscious. And just as there are different ways to be in business, there are different people suited to these models. Your job is to be honest about what you want and what makes you tick and try to ensure that you select a business model that suits your personality. After all, you'll spend most of your week at this work place.

Anyway, these are simply the main ways of being in business, of doing business and of taking money out of your enterprise. There are others, and there are hybrids of the ones I've outlined. Some will catch your eye and others will seem inappropriate. Trust your instincts on this and have some honest conversations with yourself. A business can be a full immersion exercise and it helps to start with who you really are before opting for one type of business involvement over another.

CHAPTER 10

EMPLOYEES

I have been employing people since my late twenties, when I first went out on my own and formed Bouris Dowd Vince, a law and accounting firm in Sydney. Like all employers I was not naturally good at it to begin with (not bad, either) but I've had to learn a lot of lessons about how to select the right people, how to motivate them, how to judge performance, how to build teams, and how to create an atmosphere where people of all types can feel that they're in the job that suits them.

So I see this issue of how to make a workplace deliver what you want from the perspective of an entrepreneurial employer who is looking for certain attributes and qualities. To this day I still look for people who know themselves, back themselves, are good listeners, and have the capacity to execute. These are the qualities I look for as an employer—this is how I create sustained value in my own businesses, by starting with employees with good attitudes.

But what you look for and how you arrange yourself for a position in someone else's company is a different journey. It's something you have to initiate from within because, in the end, the happiness you feel in a job, your usefulness and your capacity to achieve, are all largely dependent on what you *bring* as opposed to what the employer can *give*. Most employees who lose their way have become too interested in what is being given to them. When employees let this happen, they run the risk of losing control over what they're doing, losing touch with their colleagues, and becoming passive and fatalistic.

So whether you're trying to move upwards in your current employment or you're looking to move to a new organisation, always start with yourself and with what you bring to the business and want to achieve. All good employees begin with this honest appraisal.

WHAT SORT OF EMPLOYEE ARE YOU?

Employees and business owners are very different yet they have a few factors in common: they both operate in a market, they both have to please the people who pay them revenues, and for both employees and business owners, their performance is critical.

While there are many dynamics acting on employees, the best place to start is by gauging if you are job-centred or growth-focused. Happiness and performance are complex subjects, but in the workplace they begin with feeling that your personal attributes are matched to your work demands. If you're being asked to contribute to the future prospects of the business by working long hours, yet all you really wanted was a job, then you will be miserable. And if you're shoved in a cubicle until 5 p.m. and asked to do the same thing every day, when what you really want to do is contribute to growing the company, then you, too, will be miserable.

Neither the growth-oriented nor the job-focused person is very happy when forced to be what they're not. So before you even get to an interview, be clear on what you want: job or growth; safety or excitement; certainty or challenge.

The biggest difference between an employee and business owner in this respect is that in a business you get to state the culture of the workplace. When you start with self-evaluation techniques as an employee, you're not only judging what drives you, but what the employer wants delivered from the position itself. So employees have a matrix to apply before they see things clearly and end up in a satisfying work life: they have to know who they are, and also what the employer expects to be delivered. And then they have to make a match. Here are some things to look for.

JOB-FOCUSED EMPLOYEE

The idea of the job is fairly basic: you show up, do 40 hours a week, and are paid a set amount of salary fortnightly. Some people love working this way—others don't understand it, could never do it. However, the trick is not what the job is. The trick is to know who *you* are, that this is what *you* want, and *you* are happy doing this.

Most organisations with more than twenty employees will have more people doing 'jobs' than those pursuing growth-oriented careers. The delineating difference is that the growth-oriented position seeks to align the employee more with the agenda of the owners, whereas the job is a purchase of someone's time and, usually, expertise. The joy of job-centred employment is that when it's time to knock-off, the employee can leave their work behind. It's more relaxing and creates an easier demarcation. When people talk about rearranging themselves so they have a better work–life balance, this is what they're talking about. For people who seek growth as employees, their life is their work, and vice versa. But for job-focused people, the life is separate from the work and they can only be happy when this separation is real and sustained.

How do you know that this is who you are? Typically you:

- Say things like 'I work to live not live to work'.
- Deeply resent being called at home about a work matter.
- Make it clear to your employer that you don't do overnight work travel.
- Allow the entire organisation to know that you play sport on Saturdays.
- Avoid salary agreements that require periodic weekend work.
- Have a personal mobile phone number that no one at work has access to.

The list goes on. You get the idea. If you fit into any of these scenarios—and more—then it's likely you are a job-focused person. You do the described job, you leave at 5 p.m., you don't like to be called at home, you don't do weekends, no one messes with your yoga or footy. End of story.

I don't have a problem with this. In fact, I respect people who lay down the limits of their employment. And in my experience, the job-focused person is not likely to be any better or any worse at their job than their growth-oriented colleague. I also understand that there are occupational psychologists who say that job-focused people have better mental health precisely because they do insist on boundaries, giving them greater quality in their lives outside of the workplace.

However, there is always the question of remuneration and promotion. In many organisations it is quite clear that the owners or executives want growth-oriented people who are prepared to do what it takes to drive financial expansion, and, correspondingly, share in that growth. This is the alignment of employee with owner: making their remuneration and promotion dependent on delivering growth to the owner. This always seems to leave the job-focused person on the outer, and many an unhappy and disoriented employee who simply wanted a job has found themselves dragged into the growth system and all of the stress and overwork that goes with it.

My advice is this: if you are a job-focused person, you will not enjoy taking the growth-oriented path. But, rightly, you then ask how you keep your career trajectory and your earnings on track when you are essentially saying 'no' to insane overtime and having your phone on at all times. Here are a few tips:

- **Delivery, not hours**—If all you are selling is 40 hours a week, then you will slip back. Focus on what you deliver to the owners, rather than how many hours you sell. Stop looking at the clock!

- **Develop an expertise**—Pertaining to the first point, employees are in a marketplace, and in a marketplace you need something that the other merchants don't have. Or you have to deliver it better or cheaper. Use your time in a workplace to develop an expertise: you may not be irreplaceable, but you enhance your value if you can do something no one else can.

- **Talk upwards**—If you want to work for 40 hours and still move up in the organisation and get regular pay rises, ensure that you are talking about your work rules with the HR person, the business owners or your senior manager.
- **Peer buy-in**—While those above you have to be comfortable with what is going on, you also need your co-workers to accept that while you don't work nights and weekends, you are a big contributor to the team effort. Therefore, you need considerable . . .
- **Output**—Don't be a clock-watcher or a water-cooler lingerer or a constant smoker. Ensure that the 40 hours you do work produce solid output. The trick is that when those other team members and managers are still working on a problem at 7.30 p.m., make sure the reports or spreadsheets that you were responsible for are in their hands, with all of your notes and comments attached. Be known for what you do, not for what you don't.
- **Be constructive**—If a situation is looming where you might be required for weekend work or an off-site event, try to be constructive about how you can fit into this—or not fit in. Don't get a reputation for being stubborn or difficult.
- **Don't moralise**—The fastest way for a job-only employee to lose status and earnings is to moralise to managers or owners about how important parenting or family life or sporting

pursuits are. You think they don't have a life outside the workplace too?

- **Don't whine; sell**—Employees who complain about the work or the hours or the travel—when those around them are being asked for the same effort—will inevitably fall by the way, regardless of being job- or growth-focused. If you want to stay on a promotion track, but wall-off your family life and only work 40 hours a week, then you need to be selling your abilities and delivery, not whining about what is being asked of you.

In the end, getting ahead in employed work is about finding the right fit for your skills, outlook and priorities. But that process starts with you knowing about you. One of the saddest things I've seen in organisations is where a good person signs on for the wrong job, with the wrong demands. It changes them: confident people lose confidence; outgoing people become introverted; productive people start twiddling their thumbs. So start with yourself: be honest about who you are, what drives you and what you want. And if you can, avoid making it all about money.

CHAPTER 11

GROWTH-FOCUSED EMPLOYEES

Not every employee watches the clock and can't wait to be out of the building. They want to grow: grow sales, grow clients, grow revenues and grow their own expertise and value. They are called ambitious or go-getters, but I call them growth-focused employees and they are most suited to growth-oriented positions within their organisation.

WHAT ARE GROWTH-ORIENTED POSITIONS?

The growth-oriented position demands that the employee has a measure of responsibility for the expansion of a division, sales line, business or client-base—call it what you will. If you are offered a job in which the description comes with a written or verbal demand that a certain benchmark is reached per year or quarter, then you are in a growth job. But not all of these positions have financial benchmarks to reach. Graduates who go into law and accounting firms as associates will be asked to 'bill' a certain number of client hours per month, and growth-oriented people in government and NGO employment might be asked for performance that covers qualitative rather than quantitative measurements.

Some of these positions, in my experience, are highly specified in terms of the goals to be attained: usually sales, market share, profit, gross margin, earnings per employee, return on capital, etc. Every industry will have its own way of judging your success and every workplace will be asking you to improve upon the person you replaced, and will be suggesting that you exceed the performance of the person hired on the same day as you. In some cases, the employer expects you to do *much* better than your predecessor.

The benchmark or the goal is the first sign of a growth job; another is that you are asked to make some of your income dependent on how close you come to achieving these goals. This, of course, gives the employee incentive to cut costs, charge more for the goods or services, and work harder, or work his own staff harder.

The third aspect of the growth position is that the working hours expected of this job is the length of a piece of string. Having given you minimum benchmarks, and financial incentives, the employer now stands back and allows you to do whatever it takes. Which for most people—and yes, I've been there—means working long hours to achieve the first two components. For some people this means undertaking brutal travel regimes with no extra salary.

The growth jobs I have just described will be familiar to many readers. They exist across all industries and while we associate them with corporations and the biggest law and accounting firms, they also exist in private businesses. They are most noticeable in those industries where smart people willing to take on responsibility are rewarded with a lot of money and perks (such as holidays, cars, golf club memberships) for reaching their benchmarks: bankers, lawyers, corporate managers and venture capitalists, to name a few. But these are just the high-profile examples; these jobs also exist in large and medium-sized companies, and even suburban businesses—wherever an employer needs to make an employee feel more like an owner. And all owners look for growth: growth in sales, growth in equity, growth in market share, growth in dividends.

Increasingly, these jobs are advertised via recruitment firms because the employer knows that the price for employing the wrong person can be high. However, many growth jobs are still advertised in mainstream newspaper and website advertising, often with a rider beside the quoted salary: '$110 000 base + performance incentives.' Other advertising may be more obtuse: 'Salary $100 000—$130 000', for instance, usually means part of your income is an incentive payment, depending on reaching your growth figures.

WHO ARE YOU?

The jobs I have spelled out above are conspicuous because they carry status, responsibility and remuneration greater than other jobs. They also carry with them the chance of failure, the risk of stress-related disorders, and the real possibility that they take over your life, squeezing out other aspects such as social, family and sporting or cultural interests.

There are two ways that people come to these jobs: you either fall into the job or you seek it out. Each avenue requires a bit of thinking about whether this is what you want—as I keeping saying, when the wrong person takes a job like this, they're miserable—and each might need slightly different self-evaluation.

FALLING INTO IT

For many employees, these growth jobs are not what they sought out. They fall into them for a number of reasons. For example:

- It starts off as a job but you acquire specific skills that mean you're catapulted into a role where you're expected to run a team and meet targets.
- The person above you quits and the workload and responsibility falls to you because no one else understands the role or the work.
- The employer restructures after a management consultant comes through the building and previously job-focused roles are turned onto growth-oriented positions with benchmarks to achieve.
- You take a temporary role and it becomes permanent.

In all of these scenarios, the employee hasn't gone looking for this ambitious type of role and they are not really prepared. They either flourish under the new pressure or the new expectations can knock the confidence out of them. Some people rise to the challenge, seeking out management training, mentoring and other support, while others really cannot cope and become depressed and disengaged. There is something sad and unnecessary about seeing a person who essentially just wanted a job being thrown into 60-hour weeks and endless pressure about the performance of them and their team.

Before taking any position—either inside your current workplace or externally—I suggest you do two things:

1. Make a list of what drives you in your professional life. Don't use jargon phrases like, 'I like engaging with a team'. Get beyond the consulting talk and describe what turns you on: Making deals? Getting thanks from a client? Out-manoeuvring a rival in another company? Pitching to new customers? Seeing your company spoken about in glowing terms in the business media? Just list the things that give you a buzz. If that doesn't come naturally, write down the five times in your current or previous job when you felt uplifted and on top of your game. What were they? Is there a pattern? People who do this honestly can usually ascertain if they are suited to a growth job. It starts with knowing yourself. If you don't have excitement from any of those factors that create business growth then you might want to rethink the job offer, regardless of the money. Business growth is a river that sometimes turns into a torrent and, occasionally, a waterfall—if you're not equipped, you'll hate it.

2. Ignore the salary on offer and look at the description. When you fall into one of these positions, you usually have the advantage of already being in the organisation and being able to work out what the employer wants, how it will be measured and whether you can achieve the performance. Have a look

behind the name of the position and see what's really being asked. What's the workload? What are your resources? Have the targets ever been met?

Start with what drives you *before* worrying about what the employer wants. High salaries and big bonuses are important considerations, but they don't make the job any more interesting and they don't make you any more suited to the task. People who fall into the wrong job are letting the organisation decide who they are. But this is something you have to do for yourself.

CHASING IT

Even if the growth-oriented job is what you want, you should still do some basic self-evaluation before chasing it. When you first start in employment there can be a sense of urgency or impatience. People commit themselves to high-stress paths because that's what their university friends are doing, or that's what everyone in the firm is aiming for, or because they just want to earn the best money. In other words, many employees push themselves into positions that are growth-oriented based on ambition, money or peer pressure, but not on personal fulfilment or purpose.

I have known many unhappy people who, having thrown themselves into this career race, wonder where the years went. The truth is that when you focus a career on ambition or money, you may not be considering other core parts of yourself. You may have to make decisions about where you live, whether you start a family, how much time you get to spend playing sport—or even what kind of diet or exercise regime you end up with—by taking on some of the growth-oriented jobs. Remember, the big difference between being an employee and owning a business is that when you're an employee the company owns your time. It gets dressed up as responsibility, growth targets and bonuses, but in the end, it's your time they are buying.

Sometimes it's not the time requirements of these jobs as much as the extent of them. Many people can work 60-hour weeks for a month; most are exhausted after doing that for six months. Many ambitious people can handle four business trips a year; ten is too much for most. These are the sorts of things you can think through before committing to a growth career, and before saying yes to the bonus structure being offered.

If you have no choice, and you have to take this job, then at least know who you are and where you stand with some of the burdens of the position. As the cliché goes, forewarned is forearmed: if you make yourself aware of what you want then you can design the job description to suit you before you take it. Many organisations are surprisingly flexible about job-design, but they always wait for the candidate to ask. It's not a bad way to approach it—designing a job actually makes you seem more in charge, more responsible and a good negotiator. Generally speaking, it's ambitious women who do this, but men should do it more, too. There is nothing wrong with trying to align your professional existence with your personal needs.

The growth-oriented job is not identical to the growth-oriented business. In the job, you have all of the stress of an employer—and layers of management—looking over your shoulder, whereas when you own a growth-oriented business, the stress is of your own making, your mistakes are yours. Yes, there are politics in any organisation, but in your own business those political forces reflect your own culture; when you are ambitious as an employee in someone else's organisation, the politics are out of your control and can be quite enervating and sometimes undermining.

So ask yourself some basic questions before pursuing this sort of life:

- Can you give so much of yourself to someone else's company?
- Are you prepared for periods of your life when you see your workmates and customers more than your friends and family?
- How important is your health to you?
- While the remuneration is great, does it counter-balance the negatives?

The truth of growth-focused jobs is that more is expected of you all the time: more hours, more responsibility, more commitment, more sacrifice. I know people who breeze through these types of jobs, loving every minute of them, seeming to come alive with the competition and the hard work. But others become crushed in the never-ending demands of time, performance and responsibility. This is particularly the case with the people asked to run historically troubled divisions of an organisation or corporate divisions that are being squeezed by economic structural change.

What is the difference between those who breeze through and those who struggle? I believe it might come down to those who know themselves and use regular self-reflection to stay centred and focused. This really becomes reality in the one thing that all growth-oriented employees are asked to commit to: the bonus.

THE BONUS OR THE PURPOSE?

In the old days, growth-oriented employees were incentivised on a formula handed down from the executives. It allowed employees to make between one-tenth and one-third of their base salary in bonuses. Financial services companies, such as banks and insurance companies, still remunerate managers this way because their business models and revenues streams are largely unchanged formulas. But modern remuneration policies often allow employees to suggest their own bonus structures, based on achievements of stated goals.

In this environment, self-awareness is crucial. If you have input into how you can be judged professionally and remunerated financially, you must be thinking not only in terms of what the employer wants but what you are best able to give. This self-analysis is a critical action when you're aiming at a growth-oriented career as an employee.

The more you think about yourself in a self-critical way, the more likely you are to not just devise a bonus structure that plays to your strengths, but actually end up with a career which makes you happy because it's exactly where you should be. At the start of this book I reflected that the building blocks of a happy working life were hard work, the ability to be relentless and the identification of your purpose. It holds as much for employees as it does for business owners.

In employed life, if you want to become qualified, move up and make great income from your chosen career, then hard work and a relentless work ethic will be the norm among your peers. But the things that will keep you making career decisions that leave you fulfilled and happy about work are the ones where your true self is somehow reflected. This is about purpose: behaving in a way that the question of 'why' is answered whenever you ask it.

People who think about what makes them happy, what inspires them, when they're at their best, etc., are not narcissistic: they are balancing the external needs-driven model of the organisation with their internal desire. At best, workplace psychologists might call this a coping mechanism; I call it a tool for achieving, a way to stay sane and the first step in maintaining basic health as you push yourself to work harder and put yourself under more stress.

Purpose, far from being an airy-fairy concept, is the way that many high-achievers stay mentally fresh and focused in times of stress and overwork. It all starts with a habit of self-reflection, of constantly knowing 'why' you are doing what you're doing. This adds up to purpose and those who have it are more likely to make decisions that move them towards companies and divisions and specific employers who reflect what they're really good at.

Bonuses come and bonuses go: you grab some, you miss others. But these remuneration formulas sit at the heart of most growth-oriented employment, and while they may feel like golden carrots held out to keep you running, they are also a very good way to make you think about your purpose: Why are you doing this job? What is most important about this position? If you could improve one aspect of your responsibilities, what would it be?

These same questions that go to your purpose are also the issues that should underpin your bonus structure, if you have input into how it's designed. Sometimes people in high-achieving employed situations are tricked into thinking that they work for bonuses. Actually, if you add your own purpose to the equation, you might find that the bonus works for you.

The people who get on best in organisations are those who know themselves. It doesn't matter if you take the ambitious route and go for growth, or if you prefer to work predictable hours with low stress. The employees who are healthiest and happiest are the ones who don't allow themselves to be subsumed by the company culture or the employer's salaries. The healthiest and happiest employees begin the journey with who they are, what inspires them and what motivates them, and take that as the starting point. People who design employment around what suits their personality don't just make themselves more successful—they are also noticed and favoured by most employers.

CHAPTER 12

BUILDING A BUSINESS

I have a very simple way of building a business. I start at the exit. My starting point is the end. Many people think this sounds strange, so let me explain how it works.

I begin with the end and build a business case in reverse from there. All of the strategy I put together is informed by the requirements of the exit. I start with what the business should be or could be worth in five years, given the market, the demand, emerging technology and a few other bits and pieces that I can find out.

Once I have a possible exit price for the business, then I reverse-engineer the strategy because now I can see the key components that I need. Once I am happy with the strategy, I execute, with discipline.

This is how most business owners build an enterprise: they begin with the exit as their goal, and reverse-engineer until they have sufficient details to build a strategy. This is very different to how most amateurs or newcomers approach business: they begin with goals that often lack definition—'to sell the most coffee', etc.—then they build strategies that should lead towards these goals.

If you are new to business—or your first try was only averagely successful, or your current business needs a revamp—you should at least look at my approach. Not only is it the most common approach for successful business-builders, it is also the method of professional investors such as venture capitalists and private equity groups.

Professional business-builders and investors always start with the exit: this is the goal. They begin with a possible valuation of the business, given two or three scenarios. Then they factor time into the equation: they don't usually want to be invested in a business forever. So the goal they set is based on one of several possible valuations—at year three, year four and year five—given the input of × amount of capital and a certain management team.

Every calculation of strategy will be made around the goal of the exit. Everything they have to do for the next five or less years is reflected in that exit, from marketing to IT systems, hiring (and firing), expansions, acquisitions and recapitalisation. You name it, the decisions will be building to a point where the business is worth X, based on multiples of earnings and market position.

You can do this, too. You don't have to be a growth-oriented business owner. You can make it work if you're actually buying a job. If you're job-focused—and you want this to be a source of salary for the next twenty years—you can still base your strategy on what the business could be sold for in five years time.

It isn't that you will necessarily be building the business for a sale. Instead, you can use all of the tricks of the professional business-builder to make the business more valuable in the eyes of the market. Let's say you buy a suburban florist shop for $300 000 and from the earnings multiple applied to this shop you intend to take $100 000 per year from the earnings for yourself, with a part-time employee, rent and supply costs taking the rest. If you concentrate on reducing your costs and increasing your revenues, you can still have the business paying you a salary, but you are increasing the market value (and your equity) in the business, giving you a capital gain should you ever want to (or need to) sell.

GROWING SUCCESSFULLY

The growth-oriented business owner is building a business so it can be sold in future for much more than was invested into it. The owner is looking for the following two things: ongoing income during the building phase, and a capital gain when the business is sold. Smart business-builders manage to attain both income and appreciation from the business.

In the example we have used previously, of the growth-oriented café owner, she may have the opportunity to buy a café for $200 000, based on a price consisting of 2 × annual earnings. If she wants to build this café so she can sell it for $400 000, then she has to start with the exit—the sale price—and build back from there. What drives earnings in the café industry? What constrains earnings growth? What will she have to spend? Who will she have to hire? How long will the earnings growth take? What market is she in? What is the aggregate demand?

All of these questions hang on the exit. All of the changes that have to happen will happen because of, and in line with, the exit. And if she gets it right—doesn't rush the process or run ahead of actual demand—she will be paying herself a salary while grooming the business for sale.

If the plan works, the equation could look something like this:

Cost of business	$200 000
Capital investment	$50 000
Total cost invested	$250 000
Sale price	$400 000
Capital gain	$150 000
Salary (three years)	$150 000
Total	$300 000

As you can see, when you build a business, there are variables that alter what the ultimate equation will look like. But whether you're buying a floundering café or selling the latest in technology, there are some common factors that all business-builders should look at.

TYPES OF EXIT

The business built for sale starts with the exit, which means a sale of some kind. There can only be a sale where there is a market, so business sales usually take place in well-known formats:

- **Trade sale**—A business is listed by a business broker, business exchange or as a classified advertisement, usually in a magazine that panders to the particular industry of the business. There are also networks of accountants and solicitors, but the public doesn't see into these: your solicitor or accountant deals with the networks and tells you about the opportunities. Trade sales involve a payment for the business—at the date nominated, you own the business.

- **Distressed sale**—When a business cannot pay its creditors as and when the bills fall due, the business is insolvent. It is illegal to trade insolvently in Australia, so there are three main ways in which distressed businesses can trade-out before becoming insolvent: administration, which is when a qualified accountant takes control of the running of a distressed business on behalf of creditors, often banks; voluntary administration, when a distressed business elects administration with a firm of accountants, at which point they trade under legal guidelines; and liquidation, when the distressed company is wound up by an accountant and the assets sold (by tender or auction usually) to maximise returns to creditors.

- **Merger**—When the assets of one business are merged with another business to form one entity. Each entity is typically 'sold' into the new entity, creating dividends for the shareholders.

- **Acquisition**—When you sell your business as a going concern to another business.

- **Partial buy-out**—Part-owners of the business may sell their shares, often to other shareholders. If you sell your shares to the other shareholders, you exit the business.

- **Initial public offering**—When a privately held business issues public offer shares through the Australian Stock Exchange (ASX), and thus becomes a 'public' company. This is an exit because the people who held the shares in the private entity are selling their shares in the new entity, to the public.

VALUATION

Every single good and service on the face of the earth that you can buy has some kind of a valuation model sitting behind it. Some of the valuations you are used to, and you accept, include: petrol, houses, interest rates, oranges, lumber, iPads. These items fluctuate with supply and demand, but they rely on basic formulas.

When businesses are sold, they too have accepted valuation models, usually a formula based on an earnings multiple. Each industry has its own rule-of-thumb earnings multiple to indicate value. In some industries, the business is valued at 1 × annual earnings (earnings before interest and tax, or EBIT); in other industries the multiple is closer to 4 × or even 6 × annual earnings.

Look at the BizExchange Index, an intermediary service that among other things tracks EBIT earnings multiples for business sales in different industries. In their June 2011 Index, under the heading 'Accommodation, Cafes & Restaurants', the multiples range from low (0.75), to common (1.66), to high (3.97). Your $200 000 EBIT earning café could be offered between $150 000 and almost $800 000. That is a huge range, and obviously for the purposes of this book I've opted for a midpoint of a 2 × earnings multiple, delivering a sale price of $400 000.

What shifts these multiples around? Earnings multiples are a very good guide, but they are starting points in a discussion along with other factors.

EXTERNAL FACTORS

I start with the rule-of-thumb earnings multiple because that's where the market starts—but the market also attaches prominence to business factors, such as profit margins, stability of revenues, competitive advantage, the life-stage of the industry (upturn, downturn, etc.), and reliance of the revenues on the owner operator. There are accountants and consultants who help business-builders to get these factors to a point where they work for you rather than against you. And when you see the discrepancies between a low and a high earnings multiple for cafés and restaurants, you see why they are worth concentrating on when running your business.

Some factors you can't change, but you can absolutely work on net profit margins by ensuring good price points and discipline about your costs. Competitive advantage may take some thinking but it's worth making a feature of if you can find it (nice view, exclusive access to organic coffee, location beside a commuter rail station, earliest opener in the finance district, etc.). Ensuring that the business can operate and make good revenues without the owner being there is something that can be built up with team-building and training over a couple of years. Even the existence of a competent, full-time manager in the business can lift its value because the enterprise is not reliant on the owner in order to create revenues.

KNOW YOUR PRICE

When you build a business for growth and for sale, your exit is built on a valuation, which is built on an assumption about someone paying that price. But even if you have three or four interested parties looking over your café, will they pay the industry standard earnings multiple? Will you get your $400 000? In order to further solidify your exit strategy, you need to be smart about the market you are selling into. Is the geographic area achieving the same multiples as the industry average? Is the industry multiple relevant now or was the multiple arrived at five or ten years ago? What was the last price paid for an established café in your area and what was the multiple? As I write this, stories have appeared in the *Sydney Morning Herald* about the discrepancy between states when it comes to the price of coffee, an average of $3.30 in Sydney compared to $3.90 in Perth. Given that coffee machine maker Gilkatho says each cup of coffee contains 35 cents worth of constituent materials, the difference between $2.95 and $3.55 in your margin is actually quite large, and gives scope for adjusting your earnings, when amortised across thousands of cups of coffee sold. So it's worth investigating these differences before committing to an exit price strategy.

The price paid is one part of your market, but the other aspect is the buyer.

KNOW YOUR BUYER

Before building a business for sale, ask yourself: 'Who will buy this business for the price I want to charge?' The difference between a professional business-builder and someone who owned a business and happened to do well when they sold it is that the professional knows who the buyer is years before they sell it. This is not an arrogant claim to mystical powers, this is a reality of understanding your market that is every bit as important as understanding how the price works.

You need to know your buyer before you have met them. Anyone can ask their accountant for an industry earnings multiple that gives guidance to a business valuation along with ancillary factors. But knowing your buyer is something that won't usually happen quickly. It involves market intelligence, industry research and legwork—i.e. walking into other cafés, talking with them, asking them what's going on. Let's look at some of the aspects of knowing your buyer:

- **The me-too buyer; buying a job**—Many professional business-builders will construct their enterprises for this type of buyer, who is looking for a small business and a 'turnkey' solution: long lease, established suppliers and deliveries, café already fitted out, plant and machinery included in the business, and the right to keep trading under the name you established. They want to walk straight in and start making coffees, serving cakes and earning a salary. This type of buyer will pay a premium for a me-too business with complete books, established turnover and a solid net profit margin that shows the business makes money. If you can take all the hard work out of the business, and show predictable revenues, you will be repaid with a good sale price.
- **The start-up buyer**—The start-up business owner is unlikely to pay the premium you want for a fully developed turnkey

café. They are more likely to buy a distressed business and build it up, or start a café from scratch: they are looking for the same asset appreciation as you. If this is the market you're aiming for, then save your money and don't invest too much in capital improvements. The start-up buyer doesn't have a lot of money—the ones with money want the me-too business.

- **The competitor**—One of the common buyers for a growth-oriented business is a competitor. If you take an averagely performing business and build it into something much stronger, you could present yourself as an easy way for another company to 'buy growth'. These sorts of buyers are usually the fourth-ranked company wanting to become the second-ranked, and the fast way to build sales and revenues is to buy them. Have a look at how the computer industry has changed over the past twenty years—the participants buy one another, attempting to increase market share and sales. Other businesses that do this include insurance companies, banks, trucking firms, courier companies and trade suppliers. This is always a buyer worth focusing on because they will pay a premium above the earnings multiple in order to boost their own market share. If this is who you're aiming for, ensure that your sales or market share is in the precise field that this buyer wants to pursue. These buyers are usually looking for a client list attached to the business, so ensure that you can show repeat customers in your revenues.

NEW AND NICHE BUSINESSES

Smart business owners see a new or niche market emerging that the big corporations haven't noticed. They build a business to serve this market with sweat and debt, until the big corporation finds it easier to buy their business than to build its own. Examples include Gerry McGowan's Impulse Airlines, which pioneered low-cost regional routes and made them profitable before Qantas bought the business from him in 2001. Gatorade started as sports drink for American football players and is now Pepsico's fourth-largest selling product. OzEmail was formed as an internet service provider when few people in Australia knew what one was or even sent emails. It was sold in 1999 to US telecom giant WorldCom.

Niches attract larger buyers, whether the business is on a small or large scale. If your potential buyer is a niche buyer—or you think they might be—think about what they want, how they want it and what price they will pay to have it. If this is your buyer, you must have uniqueness: there was only one Gatorade, OzEmail was the first in Australia (and therefore had the most customers), and Impulse Airlines did what Qantas had been unable to do (make money from a low-cost airline). Making your business the target of a niche buyer does not mean you have to be earth-shatteringly unique or innovative. It requires, simply, that you have built something that the larger player needs.

TECHNOLOGY-DRIVEN BUSINESSES

Your exit strategy can also be built on a technology which is sufficiently rare, unique or good at what it does; one that a larger business will want to buy from you, just to have that technology. This is a relatively common occurrence but it's also an exit strategy that can totally miss its mark. Before investing money in your business, you will have to invest in building your technology, and getting it working so its utility can be judged. Be very clear that a market exists for this technology. If you get it right, you can be rewarded with a large sale price. But if there's not a clear commercial use, there's no market; and if there's no market, there won't be a buyer of the type you envisage. So, when it comes to technology-driven businesses, you need to do lots of homework.

Because the development of the business starts with the exit, and what you want to be paid, it really is worth spending some time on this part of your planning. Accountants can be very useful for identifying who the buyer might be and what multiple they will pay, based on which factors are present in the business. They will also help you craft your financial performance so that any prospective buyer will be motivated. However, these are basics that you—the owner—has to understand instinctively. The entire rationale of building this business is to have it worth × dollars on a certain date. You cannot outsource this knowledge or the daily focus on it. You have to start doing your homework.

CHAPTER 13

GETTING STARTED— THE BUSINESS PLAN

Let's say you have narrowed down your exit to how the business should value-up and what buyer you are most likely to get this price from. Setting this goal is the most important part of the business, in my opinion, because it shows you the shape of the evolving business and acts as a beacon.

But now you need a plan for getting there. You need a strategy. The strategy itself is a cross between a road map and an instruction book, with a strong sense of narrative. All narratives have a beginning, a middle and an end—and your business strategy is no different. It should tell a story about how you are getting from *here* to *there*, with a story in between of how the battles are to be fought and won. A good business strategy should be no longer than two pages, and it can either be written in paragraphs, like a story, or it can be simplified to look more like a list of steps. Both, if they're clear and make sense, can operate as a business plan.

Many people who are opening their first business focus on the business plan in the wrong way or, should I say, they focus on the business plan in a way that isn't going to help them or the business: they concentrate on how it looks rather than on how it reads; they focus on charts and graphs rather than what drives the trend lines in those pictures; they fall back on jargon when clear expression is required; they resort to grandiose claims about paradigm shifts and game-changers rather than explain how to lift sales by their forecast 10 per cent per annum; and almost without fail they focus on the format and layout of the document rather than its content. I like a well laid out document as much as anyone. But the business plan is really about content, and it must do one thing above all: it must answer the questions.

WHAT ARE THE QUESTIONS?

Earlier in this book I spoke about attitude and outlook, and I referred to a way of seeing the world in which you never accept the status quo. Your business exists in a dynamic, ever-changing environment and complacency is dangerous. The best method I know of to avoid complacency and join the dynamic flow is to keep asking the questions.

What are the questions? These are the issues that you have asked of yourself in response to what the market is telling you. The questions cover the general: What is the target? What is the plan to get there? Who are the key personnel? Is it achievable given the market? The questions also cover the more specific: the SWOT (strengths, weaknesses, opportunities and threats) analysis is essentially a series of responses to questions you asked of yourself. And the questions also go deeper, to micro-responses that you've worked on as your self-questioning has uncovered problems in your strategy. For instance, what will my cost of capital do to my net profit margin if I have to borrow to upgrade this business? If expansion to new sites is part of the plan, will this create a drag on my margin by duplicating too many costs? What upgrade can I make to the business that produces scale rather than cost duplication?

Specifically, every business owner should have challenged themselves with some basic questions before buying or forming a business and seriously setting a target. These questions—and their answers—must be embedded in the business plan. They include:

- What is the aggregate demand for what I want to sell?
- What is the market price for what I am selling?
- Does the location of my business alter demand and price?
- Which factors influence my costs?
- Is my business constrained in its sales volume? What are the constraints?
- What part does economic growth, interest rates and inflation play in demand?
- What have equivalent businesses sold for recently?
- Is my expertise sufficient to meet market demand?
- What novel features or competitive advantages do I bring to this industry?
- Who or what can undermine my plans for growth?

My own business plans start with one page of assumptions and then five pages of planning. The assumptions tell me the state of the market, and the price of the goods I sell and how many I can sell. Assumptions are macro factors—such as gross domestic product (GDP) and inflation—as well as smaller things like the cost of wages and an office lease.

I believe all the best strategies are informed by questioning. There's an argument to be made that when committing the strategy to a business plan, the only plan worth reading is the one that answers questions of the type I've used above. Putting this another way: imagine your business plan has found its way to a venture capitalist and he has given you an hour of his time. You sit down and over the next 60 minutes this experienced, successful investor in businesses just like yours takes apart your business plan piece by piece. He will do this by doing what any investor, experienced business person or banker will do with a business plan: challenge its assumptions by asking questions.

If you can't answer the questions asked by this person then you haven't done your job and your business plan is obviously still a work in progress. I can't emphasise this enough: ask the questions of your own assumptions before you go into business; challenge yourself before the market challenges you.

This goes equally for the staples of business planning, such as a SWOT analysis. The analysis of strengths, weaknesses, opportunities and threats is certainly something that should be in a business plan, but does it have to be in its own box at the end of the document? So many newcomers to business do this, and it looks like denial, as if shifting the self-challenging questions to the back of the document renders them irrelevant, or not as powerful as the growth scenario in the middle. The SWOT should actually be a series of questions you ask of yourself and your business, rather than a list of answers. For instance, if your new venture is a law firm, start with something like: 'What is my strength in providing legal advice to clients?' Then follow it up by questioning your own answer: 'Is this really a strength?', 'How could it be a greater strength?', 'Who else has this strength, and what do they charge for it?'

You should do this ongoing questioning before you have a final business plan. It will help you to construct detailed explanations of growth rather than hopeful forecasts. Let's say you list as an opportunity: 'Upgrading the manufacturing plant and machinery will allow us to produce steel fabrications faster and cheaper.' I wouldn't write that: I would take that idea as a first step and spend several weeks questioning it. What value is created by fabricating steel faster? Who else has access to these machines? How long will the advantage last? What are my capital costs to upgrade? Do the capital costs eat into my larger margin on steel fabrication sales? What does that do to my revenues? And on and on.

My questions would push me further and further into my goal of establishing an exit price for this business. So my final approach to new machinery would come from the goal itself: the EBIT (earnings before interest and tax). The opportunity would be connected directly to it and would read something along the lines of: 'The goal of doubling revenues in five years can be assisted by the purchase of new machines that increases sales by speeding manufacturing time by 22 per cent.'

The same goes for the strengths, weaknesses and threats. Anything you can identify must not only be questioned but must be questioned against the ultimate business goal. So, given that business is a constant process of questioning, your business plan has to have those questions reflected in it.

WRITING THE PLAN

I have seen thousands of business plans in my life. Most of them are crap. There are accountants and management consultants who charge new business owners thousands of dollars to write these things, and often they are useless. They might even be worse than useless because they're tricking the owner into thinking that this neatly bound ream of paper is actually going to help them. Generally, it won't ... although there are notable exceptions.

All real business plans start with the exit, and are driven by this event. And all real business plans are informed by questions.

A good business plan starts with a business valuation—or a valuation scenario—and works back from that position. They start with this exit scenario and very simply explain what has to happen in the business, over the next five or whatever years, to meet that target. The explanation is clear because of the hundred questions that have been asked before any words were written.

KEY PERFORMANCE INDICATORS (KPIs)

The best business plans make their case and grab my attention on the first page: all the numbers are there, pointing to the goal. And the way that the numbers point to the goal is by breaking the journey into small steps, which are weekly or monthly hurdles known as key performance indicators (KPIs). Each KPI is a brick, and in the telling of the story, a brick wall is built.

Let's go back to our café example again: your plan should be a few very simple benchmarks you have to reach in order to sell this business for more than you bought it, or more than it cost to establish. You can't aim for the ultimate goal every day—that could easily become meaningless or demoralising. So you break the goal into measurable steps and set yourself one main KPI—and perhaps two minor KPIs—which have to be attained every week to build the business to the ultimate target.

Your earnings multiple in the café industry is 2 × annual gross revenue—this is your valuation scenario. So to take your new business from the $200 000 valuation at which you bought it to the $400 000 price you want to sell it for, in five years time, you have to double your revenues (or increase revenues by 1.5 × and reduce costs). Doubling your sales becomes one of your benchmarks.

So the business plan should take us on a journey from the money invested in the business, through a doubling in sales, to the exit price. The journey to this benchmark will be informed by KPIs that plot the growth, so your main KPI will be cups of coffee sold per week.

If the business you've bought is selling 500 cups of coffee per week, that is your starting KPI. Every week you are trying to shift that KPI towards 1000 cups of coffee per week. Many first-time business owners will spend thousands of dollars on fancy software packages to 'track' these KPIs and make pie charts out of them. I'm sure they're useful, but tracking your main KPI from its starting point to your target is something you can easily do on a spreadsheet in your laptop or even written down in an exercise book. If you're trying to lift cups of coffee sold from 500 per week to 1000, you don't want to get too complicated. Every Sunday night just log the number you've sold.

In a smaller business, the KPI for growth will almost always be sales. Specific industries such as professional services will also measure things such as revenue per client; trade services will measure the spread of clients so the bulk of revenue is not tied up in one or two clients. Profit margin is also a good KPI because it ensures that your activity is actually making money.

Just about every growth business revolves around doing something faster, cheaper or at greater volume. These concepts will probably form a support strategy for increasing the main KPI, and they will therefore be integral to the business plan. With your café, if the aim is to double the annual earnings, the question that needs to be answered is: how can you be cheaper, faster or produce greater volumes?

So your business plan will probably answer the main question of how to increase unit sales, with an investigation of the business drivers that contribute to that central KPI. The following are some common drivers.

MAKE TIME WORK

Time can work for you, or work against you. If you look around the neighbourhood in which your café operates and see that most cafés open at 8 a.m. and close at 4 p.m., and are closed on Sundays, then you are already looking at an opportunity to increase business revenues from your use of time. The business-builder looks at this and sees the advantage: if you open at 6.30 a.m.

and close at 5, you extend your trading hours by fifteen hours per week and also create a point of difference among your rivals. If the business you bought sells 30 cups of coffee and twenty cookies per hour, the fifteen hours per week you just reclaimed has boosted your sales already.

SIZE COUNTS

Let's say you buy a café that seats 25 people. With a slight redesign of the premises, you can seat 35. You are now expanding the potential coffee and food sales volume by ten customers, because you're increasing the capacity of the café. The renovation will cost money, and this needs to be in the business plan, but with ten extra seats—each one turning over three times in two hours—you have increased your sales potential and are closer to your goal.

THINK VOLUME

To account for the longer hours and more seats, you invest in larger, better espresso machines and larger food cabinets, with extra storage in the back and a larger dishwasher. It means you can handle the increased hours and customers, rather than creating bottlenecks and turning away customers. The volume that your business turns over each week should aim to be a fairly perfect balance of your supply and demand. But the business-builder wants to grow the sales and revenues, and to get there you must invest in the capacity to grow volume.

THE RIGHT STAFF

Will one extra person—at the peak time—be worth the investment? The business plan should calculate employment expenditures against the expected gains: with all businesses there is a point at which the projected volume of sales has to be supported by more people. It's a cost of business and it's always a cost of being a business-builder. If you want to boost the earnings of this business so you can sell it for a large capital gain, the business plan must establish when extra staff are required—and then you need to invest in the best people you can find.

QUALITY

The question of finding the best people raises the issue of quality as a driver of your main KPI: sales. It is depressingly common for business owners to go over their budgets on premises, stationery, vehicles and fit-outs, then try to save money on the overhead that really delivers quality to customers—people.

Look at your café: every day it sells itself as a place to start the day or take a break, with a warm drink, a bite to eat, and a comfortable environment where someone can read a newspaper or have a chat. The key elements in this proposition are beverage, food, friendliness and décor. Unfortunately for the café owner who doesn't like to spend on wages, the décor is only one-quarter of what is being sold to customers, and is therefore just one-quarter of what drives their sales and revenues. The other three drivers of sales involve having good people on board: a barista, a cook and friendly service staff.

So remember that some businesses have to be promoted on *qualitative* grounds (experience, emotions, feelings) rather than on *quantitative* (cost, size, etc). The qualitatively driven businesses are usually service businesses, and spending money on the people who can deliver this is an investment in your business.

CREATING SCALE

Now let's bring these growth concepts together and express the journey from the starting point to the exit as an exercise in creating scale: at what point does a dollar invested produce the earnings required to reach the earnings goal? Remember, the goal is the exit price, and the exit price is established as a multiple of earnings. So, how much capital invested creates the added revenues you want? How much bigger do you have to make your operation in order to double revenues?

This quest for scale should mean a marginally greater return on the investment than simply the amount of the investment itself. For instance, if you increase your annual budget for the café by $50 000 in order to extend your hours, buy bigger espresso machines, redesign the floor space and employ extra staff, then you don't want a return of $50 000 in revenues: you want this expenditure to double the revenues from $100 000 to $200 000, because this is your exit plan.

Scale is not unlike the idea of 1+1=3, and it is one of the great dividing lines between the job-focused business owner and the growth-oriented business-builder: a person who has bought himself a job is content to take back in salary what he invests into business improvements. But the business-builder will not sleep until she finds the point where she can drive a scale operation, where one dollar invested returns two dollars in sales. Keep an eye on scale, because it's scale that enables growth.

NET PROFIT MARGIN

Most consultants or accountants will sooner or later ask their business-owner clients to focus on net profit margin as a KPI.

The net profit margin is calculated by this formula: net income ÷ revenue × 100. This gives you a number that reflects the ratio of revenues to the cost of generating the revenues. A net profit margin of 5 is not good; a net profit margin of 25 is healthy.

Working out your net profit margin is a good exercise to conduct every time you have the numbers, which for most business owners will be your quarterly business activity statement (BAS). Finance professionals become fixated on margin because this measurement not only tells you if the business activities are actually making money, it tells you how vulnerable you are to slackening sales or a rise in costs.

I think margin is an excellent KPI for business owners who have bought a job—they pay themselves the margin, so the net profit margin is virtually the yield on an investment, and is therefore a very important KPI. But business-builders should not follow margin too closely, especially where it scares them off committing to growth expenditure. To grow a business, you need to invest in it, and margin may drop for several quarters while you spend what has to be spent to build scale. However, net profit margin comes back into focus again a year before you sell: remember your buyer? They'll want solid margin, because they're buying a job.

PAYING THE PRICE

When people are new to business, they can often be lured into thinking that price is the easy road to take. In the café example, there will be owners who make the price per cup, or the price per cookie, the KPI for reaching their goal. Changing the price of your goods and services is tempting because it looks so basic on paper: if you increase the coffee price from $3.30 per cup to $3.60, you increase your margin.

But if you look around at your competitors in your neighbourhood, you'll probably notice that there is a 'market price' for the staples of café food and beverage (the cost of a coffee and cookie does not exceed $5 in the neighbourhood where I buy coffee). A similar market price exists at florists, bakeries, pubs, newsagents and butchers. A market is where supply finds demand, and a price is struck. So you have to accept the risk that in raising prices above the industry norm (or outside the accepted range) you may lose customers. Unless you know something that the rest of the industry doesn't, then avoid forcing your KPIs with price rises. It's much harder to win back a customer who has left than to win them in the first place.

The same risk attaches to price cuts. If you drop your coffee from $3.30 per cup to $3, you may increase customers by 10 per cent but you lose a similar amount of profit margin. What if the people who come for your cheap coffee only buy coffee? You'll still be paying your staff the same amount, the monthly lease will not reduce, and coffee is a global commodity so you pay what everyone else is paying for it. So you lose in margin what you gain in volume, but perhaps you also need to hire another person to deal with the morning rush. And all you gained were the customers who go for the cheapest coffee—they're not buying your expensive cookies or banana bread.

If you have inside information or access—or you have cost-reducing systems or technology—then price strategies can work. But you have to be clear before you commit to them and ask yourself: Will this hurt my margin? Will this erode my customer base?

ADVANCING TECHNOLOGY

One of the most powerful drivers in a business plan is new, advanced, hard-to-get or repurposed technology. SEEK, the Australian employment website, started migrating job classifieds online in the late 1990s because they could post endless numbers of jobs and resumes and use search algorithms so that both employers and job-seekers could find one another in the one market. The KPI of SEEK's early success was daily numbers of jobs listed, but it was technology that allowed them to keep the listing cost down while increasing the choices, which drove the listings.

Henry Ford did something similar in selling cars. His aim was to out-sell his rivals with the Model T, which he achieved by charging less for it. This was made possible because of a new technology called the production line.

Your business planning is the place for doing some really detailed cost–benefit analysis on the technology that you think is going to give you a price, access or quality advantage. But you have to be hard on yourself. I used the examples above to point to the fact that good technology drives a KPI such as sales volume or cost per unit; the technology is usually not the hero itself. If you have a digital ordering/point of sale (POS) system for your café, what will it do? Keep costs down? Drive sales? Turn over customers faster? Make financial statements easier? We're back to questions again, which is crucial when evaluating how technology can drive your business.

•

This type of business planning involves hard work as you test lots of scenarios to see if they contribute to your main KPI. If they do work, your plan should fit onto two pages and should include some simple goals for growing your revenues (the main KPI), as well as secondary KPIs which support the main target. For instance, benchmarks for number of cups sold each week; benchmarks for cost-per-sale; benchmarks for gross margins on the items you sell.

The business plan takes all of these growth scenarios and puts them against what has to be spent in order to reach the exit price. Making honest appraisals of what it costs to reach your target is crucial in the planning stage. A good plan needs these basic bricks of growth because these are the things that can be changed.

And another tip: in business, you always sweat the small stuff. You always ask the questions. That's where the growth is—that's where the capital gain is hiding when you come to sell.

CHAPTER 14

RUNNING A BUSINESS

You've set a goal and you've developed the strategy in a written document. Now you have to execute—you have to commit to the task of taking this business from the starting line to the finish. I think all three stages of the business—goal, strategy, discipline—are important, but this last one is obviously the physical test of everything else. This is the part of business life where you become fatigued, where you doubt yourself, consider giving up, wonder why you ever did this.

It's also one of the few endeavours a person can undertake where their efforts are returned in direct proportion to what they put in. It can be highly rewarding and personally fulfilling.

There are a few aspects to consider in the running of a business, although one of them starts before you open your doors. One of the clichés of business ownership is that it's better to ask questions of the business before the business has the chance to ask questions of you. Simply put, this means that the process of continual and exhaustive questioning is best started in the goal and planning stage, because it's here that many of your key assumptions can be test-bedded with calculations, industry intelligence and modelling. If you don't test the plan in the planning phase, the business gets to throw the tough questions at you once you're committed to running it. And that can be a lonely place.

While good planning is essential before you open, you eventually enter the arena—and that's when the fun starts. Let's look at some of the essentials for running a growth business.

BUSINESS STRUCTURES

Every business in Australia is operated through a structure recognised by the Australian Taxation Office. The main ones are public incorporated entity, private proprietary company, partnership, trust and sole trader. Each of these structures has its advantages and has its relevance to the owners depending on the size and the circumstances of the business. Here's a rundown of the main structures:

- **Public companies** can issue shares and raise money from the public on the Australian Stock Exchange; this allows them to capitalise with large amounts and run higher debt levels than a private company. But they are also heavily regulated and must continually disclose their financial position to the public.
- **Private proprietary companies** are a type of 'limited liability' company, so-called because the liability of the shareholders

is limited to the amount they have paid for their shares. This is the most common form of incorporation for private companies and carries the acronym 'Pty Ltd' after the name. The shareholders are the owners and the entity is managed by directors; there can be no more than 50 shareholders and they can't issue shares to, or accept deposits from, the public. Proprietary companies are fairly simple structures and many business owners use them because their accounting and tax reporting requirements are well known. Some of the red tape can be annoying but, because of these companies' legal status, the directors usually avoid being sued personally for the actions of the company. Proprietary companies do not need to publicly disclose their financial performance.

- **Partnerships** are highly flexible because the articles of association do not need to be written down, unlike a proprietary company. Some professions (for example, lawyers) use partnerships because they are not allowed to incorporate. Among like-minded professional peers, it's considered a good way to pool capital and workloads. Like proprietary companies, there's no need for a partnership to publicly disclose its financial performance.

- **Trusts** are legal entities that can be private or public. I'm talking about the private ones known as 'discretionary trusts', which are often used to own assets on behalf of family beneficiaries. This includes the shares in a proprietary company, when the company is a family affair and income needs to be spread around family members for tax purposes. Trusts are founded with deeds, and they can be altered to suit the needs of the entity.

- **Sole proprietorships** usually involve a single person in the business, utilising their own expertise to create income. There are no legal requirements of formation—as there are with partnerships, trusts and proprietary and public companies—but even if you're simply trading under your own name, you must have an Australian Business Number (ABN) and a Tax File Number (TFN).

The relevance of structure, as to size, usually goes like this— Larger businesses will seek a public listing as a public company so they can raise large amounts of capital and debt. Proprietary companies would usually be turning over at least $300 000 to make the compliance worth it, and they can be as large as $100 million turnover. Partnerships can be two people or twenty, and usually bring together people of the same profession with similar goals. Discretionary trusts are relevant to family ownership of a business. Sole proprietorship is used by those who contract their services via themselves and their own names.

The costs of each structure are a mix of the fees you pay to governments and their agencies, the fees you pay to solicitors and accountants, and the time you spend dealing with red tape. This is an evaluation you should look at before making a decision.

ADVISERS AND EXTERNAL EXPERTS

Before getting to the excitement of running an enterprise, every business owner should have at least half an hour of advice from a professional, usually an accountant or solicitor. Even if you are a sole trader, you will need someone to brief you on your legal and tax liabilities and perhaps to give you some simple advice about how to keep basic financial books. It is worth remembering that the tax law of Australia does not give free passes for ignorance or incompetence, and even honest mistakes attract reassessments with penalty rates and short timeframes in which to pay them.

Any business structure bigger than sole trader will require legal and accounting advice from the date of inception, so that you operate within the law and without creating a tax liability greater than it has to be. Trusts require deeds and trustee documents; proprietary companies require constitutions, minutes and appointments of public officer and secretary; and partnerships require agreements to be drawn up with recognition of rights, remuneration and management duties.

It's not the most interesting part of doing business, but it's the foundation and you should get it right. You don't want to be sitting around in five years time with a huge tax liability and wondering why you didn't get proper structuring and tax planning advice. There is also the question of the liability of being sued, which can be dealt with by proper structuring and alienating your personal assets from your business structure.

SOLICITORS AND ACCOUNTANTS

Not all businesses are formed from scratch: if you buy a business, you need a solicitor and accountant to make the transaction, which will typically entail buying the 'business' from the vendor's 'company' structure with your new (or existing structure). The questions of what you buy from a vendor (the business assets) and what you don't (the company entity with its tax and legal liabilities) is not something you should leave to chance and you should use experts to conduct the terms of this transaction.

Solicitors and accountants come in all sizes and fee structures and you should ask them about who they usually deal with: some have industry specialities and some focus on certain business sizes or types, such as franchises or family businesses. The goal is to find one who matches your circumstance and need.

OTHER EXTERNAL EXPERTS

While solicitors and accountants form the basic layer of external expert advice in most enterprises, there are others who you will have to engage, dependent on the nature of your business. While you can employ someone to augment your own skills and to drive the business, there are many functions in a business that are specialised and you won't be qualified to handle them. As an overall comment on your external advisers, I suggest business owners steer clear of engaging someone because they are friends of your bookkeeper's husband. This is a big mistake for first-time business people: to confuse social networks with business, which in turn confuses social obligations with commercial reality.

Your external experts must be treated as costs to your business, which deliver benefits. But there are different types of benefit. And if hiring these people comes down to budget constraints, then you'll have to prioritise them: there are experts who can help you drive sales (a marketing person); experts who establish financial and computer systems (accountants, IT consultants); and experts who establish risk mitigation, such as insurance brokers.

How you prioritise different levels of spending is dependent on what type of business you have and what is most important. What is essential—regardless of what priority they take up—is finding someone who fits with your business and delivers what they say they'll deliver. Learn to talk with other business owners, and learn to never say 'yes' to a new expert at first meeting.

So, having said this, what are some of the experts you should engage?

- Most start-up or growth businesses will need a **marketing professional**: this person will either be at the minimal technical end of the spectrum (designing logos, letterhead and business cards) or they could provide the full range of services (creating marketing plans, brochures, events and advertising). These people will carry your hopes and dreams on their service and will be contributing to the sales increase, so it's worth finding one who can deliver what you want, at a price you can afford. To find such a marketing person, go back to your questions: ask other business owners; or if you see some marketing work that catches your eye, find out who did it and track them down.

- Another expert you'll see more of than you perhaps want to is your **IT consultant**. Most businesses—even sole traders—rely on email, internet, accounting software and point of sale (POS) processing systems, all of which run on computers. It's not realistic to do business in the modern economy and not be connected. Again, ask around and come up with a short list. If you're unclear about how an IT consultant works, then put it around the other way and a send the prospective consultant a written brief of what you need. Issue a list of requirements: this makes the consultant focus on delivery rather than on work.

- Because most businesses will also borrow money, I suggest you at least look into a finance broker (more of this below). But one expert I urge all business owners to contact—even if just for a preliminary chat—is an **insurance broker**. While there are many exciting aspects of running a business, something we all have to guard against is physical risk: of fire, of losing a key employee, of theft, of our own ill health bringing the business to a halt and leaving employees out of pocket. Here's a tip: most newcomers have no idea which business insurances they should have and what they should pay for them, and anyone who's been in business for a few years has an insurance broker. Do you know how to negotiate a business interruption policy? If not, get a broker and ensure you are covered.

Other experts could include logistics companies, fit-out builders, vehicle maintenance firms, commercial laundries and all the ancillary services that can help you run your business. The only real test of cost–benefit from these service providers is whether they contribute to revenues or guard against losing them; and if they don't do either of these things, do they provide a service that could be done by someone you already employ?

DEBT AND EQUITY

Just about all businesses and all adult individuals operate under a mix of debt and equity. That is, they have a balance between what they own (equity) and what they owe (debt). There is nothing inherently 'good' about one, or 'bad' about the other. Both have to be working for you in a business, and if you can organise it so that that your debt builds equity, then you are on the right track.

DEBT

Just about every business needs debt, and a business planning on doubling its sales will probably need to borrow to do it. It's more efficient to assess what you'll need in the first six months, and plan for it, than it is to get to week four and be rushing to the bank in a panic. This is why it is worth listening to your accountants when they talk about the need for forecasting and for profit and loss budgets which are converted to cash budgets. This is the kind of planning that allows you to set up a debt facility with the bank in advance of your needs. Nevertheless, when running a business you do what you have to do.

Given that you need to borrow, a couple of tips: term loans that are secured by property you own are the cheapest way to borrow for your business. Unsecured borrowing is relatively expensive and there is no guarantee you'll get the loan, although, if you do it'll be because your owner's equity is so strong (when business lenders make unsecured loans they evaluate your debt–equity ratio). One form of unsecured borrowing is debtor finance: if you have a large receivables file with regular clients on terms, you can 'sell' these invoices to a financier, and draw-down up to 80 per cent of their value. The same financiers will also advance loans based on the inventory you hold, as long as you can prove a history of 'stock turns' and a good order book.

Be aware that debtor and inventory finance lenders will look at your equity position. If your business is small, and you don't employ a person in the finance function, I urge you to make one of your expert advisers a finance broker. They stand in the market, deal with the lenders and take a management load off your own shoulders—and they usually pride themselves on getting you the best deal.

EQUITY

Debt should be used to fund growth: it's what you borrow and it's a liability. But equity is what you own of the business value. Equity is defined as the residual value of assets in the business after you subtract liabilities. It's your wealth, expressed in the business. Be careful of claiming that the capital you seeded the business with at the start is equity. It's not: this seed capital is a liability against the business and, as such, it reduces your equity.

In most private company businesses, equity is not as important as it is in public companies because it is tightly held and the beneficiaries of the equity are also the owners. But equity does have its role: it is the counterweight to debt. When your debt levels equal or surpass your equity, it is a signal to rein in expenditure and curtail borrowing. It is also one of the measurements that commercial lenders will look at when deciding if your business is healthy.

Lenders have a phrase for owners' equity: they call it 'hurt money' and they like to see more of it rather than less. In the eyes of a lender—or an investor—the owner's equity represents blood, sweat and tears. It is the sum total of the battle to keep costs down and sales up, and most successful business owners will do almost anything to see it is not eroded.

Equity can be increased—and the health of the business improved—by the business paying back all or some of the seed capital to the investors. And while earnings are the benchmark for a business sale, equity is also looked at by prospective buyers. If there is low equity, a prospective buyer might want to know if this is because you've been taking cash out of the business, or the business is too debt-laden, or the costs are too high or the operations are inefficient. Your owner's equity will be important if a business partner or co-shareholder wants to buy you out because it raises the value of your portion. Equity is also known as 'risk capital' which is the shareholders' weekly scorecard as to the wealth they hold in the business.

CAPITAL

The most important driver for a business that has to grow is capital. I usually divide this into human capital and cash. If you want to shift the market value of your business so that you make a substantial profit when you sell it, you will need to invest cash and people into the enterprise. The most common ways of getting cash into the business to fund growth is via debt or by sale of your equity to a new investor. Hence, debt and equity are the different ways of getting the cash to you.

CHAPTER 15

BUILDING YOUR TEAM

There is an image, built up by the movies, of the business owner as a cigar-chomping tyrant who makes his decisions alone and hands out instructions to his minions with a grunt. This idea of the lone-wolf genius basically hinges on a person who is so much smarter than everyone else that he has to bear the burden of building a business or a career on his own, in constant conflict with mediocre types who would hinder his progress. It's a nice story, and it's total rubbish.

All the businesses worth talking about have reached their potential—and are still growing—because the people who started them understood the power of a good team. Whether it's Bill Gates or Steve Jobs or Henry Ford or Rupert Murdoch, anyone who wants to build a successful business has to attract, motivate and reward good people.

In the past twenty years, all large corporations and professional services firms have invested in their HR functions as they seek to ensure they have smart, qualified, skilled employees who can contribute to the goals and aspirations of the organisation. You can read estimates on the problems of employing the wrong person: the number generally comes down to a year's salary being what you lose out in termination costs, lost recruitment costs and loss of productivity during replacement.

However, employing the wrong person and having to terminate them is only one problem. There's also the problem of the person who burrows into the organisation and stays even though he's doing a below-par job. These people—who may be liked by everybody—can be a far greater drain on your business than the people who are clearly not adequate and have to be moved on. Other issues include: criminality such as embezzlement and fraud; personal problems such as alcoholism; personality clashes with the existing team or with a major client; and inability to do the job.

A large organisation can absorb these situations, to a certain degree. But private businesses cannot. Even franchises, which have manuals on how to attract the right people and give them the right training, inevitably employ someone who is wrong for the business.

Most private business owners have an added problem, and that is they can't afford to create a simply negative policy for employment to ensure they don't employ badly. They need to do it the other way around. They need to focus on growth first and risk second. So they have to find a way to attract good people rather than just how to avoid the bad.

In order to employ well, you have to find access to a talent pool, do your homework and make all of your employing decisions align with your business goals. But, most of all, you have to start with a clear picture of what your business needs. Here are the basics I look at.

JOB DESCRIPTION

When I look back on some of the poorer employment decisions I've made, it usually comes down to my own failure to clarify the requirements of the job and what kind of person would be right for it. Most of us have been raised seeing jobs advertised as a 'position' to be 'filled'. That means there is a pigeon-hole in an organisation that needs to be filled with a person who has the right qualifications and required years of experience. It's quite bureaucratic.

When you're starting a business, this might have to be turned around, so that rather than talking about a position to be filled, you talk about what the business needs right now. Rather than saying the position to be filled is group accountant, you talk in terms of the business needing a finance professional who can help stabilise a growth-business so the growth doesn't derail it. Define the job in terms of what the business needs rather than the name of the position. It may not come to you naturally, but you can make a habit of it.

THE RULES

Every employee is engaged by your business under laws, union awards and regulations as to their rights and obligations, and yours, too. You must comply with these regulations and in order to make sure you do, there are manuals you can get from government departments, unions and industry associations that spell out what you have to pay, what hours your people can work, what you have to do with superannuation and what kind of environment you have to maintain in terms of health and safety, conflict resolution and interpersonal relationships, such as bullying and sexual harassment. There's a lot to know!

You may need an expert to help you get it right. If you belong to an industry association, they usually have online resources and FAQs, as well as hotlines where you ring an industrial relations expert with your query. Some business owners use lawyers and accountants to set up their employment systems, especially if they operate in industries such as mining, oil and gas exploration and construction. These industries have complex requirements as to site and plant inspections, OH&S certification and insurance policies. It's worth getting them right or you could find your business shut down or liable for paying for damages. In these industries it's also worth remembering that the unions are part of your employment calculations.

TALENT POOLS

Your search for new employees will really start with identifying talent pools—groups of people with qualifications and a desire to work—and then working out how to access them. For instance, if you need a professional to take charge of the financial controls at the centre of your business, your identified talent pool for that employee would be accounting firms, banks and the finance controllers at businesses just like yours. If you don't want to do the driftnet approach of putting an ad in the employment websites, you should start with listing the talent pools that can provide experienced, qualified people who are already working. Then you have to access these pools . . .

ADVERTISING

I consider this to be the second resort. If you decide to advertise, you have several options. You can pay for advertising on SEEK, which will give you a national and international reach. Metro newspapers will give you a narrower reach, but probably a more qualified pool; that is, people not actively looking for a job (it sounds counter-intuitive, but generally people in work are more sought after). You can advertise in a local or regional paper, which narrows your reach even further but means your time is not wasted by people who live on the other side of the country. And finally, you can advertise with an industry magazine or its website, and narrow your search to people who clearly and precisely fit the talent pool you need.

All of these options will require you to sift through emails and letters, trying to make sense of who will get an interview. It can take up a lot of time, it is a bit of a lucky dip, and because you're not professional at this, you might have worded the advertisement incorrectly or suggested a too-low salary, which has meant most of your target audience has not bothered to contact you. In this case, you can hire a professional to do the search for you.

RECRUITMENT AGENCIES

Recruitment agencies do the advertising and the legwork and will produce for you a list of prospects that fall within the criteria you stipulated. Then it's up to you to do the interviews and selection, which the recruitment person will attend if you ask them to. This service can cost several thousand dollars and while it can be helpful, there are drawbacks.

For a start, you have to bring the recruitment person up to speed on your business and the expectations for what the employee will bring to the business. Secondly, the recruitment person may not have access to the talent pools you need, and even worse, they may prefer to do their candidate nominations primarily from their own candidate databases.

The most essential aspect of using a recruitment agency is that you stay in control of who it is you want and what they bring to your growth strategy. You have to learn to differentiate between what your business needs, and who the agency wants you to employ. They are not always the same thing.

PEER NETWORKS

The fastest and most efficient access to your employment talent pools will always be peer networks. Professional recruiters know this, which is why they infiltrate LinkedIn, Twitter and Facebook: they know peers will lead them to the right people. So if you already have a few good employees onboard, use them to find other people like them. When some names come up, ask yourself what the person can do for the business and why they would be right for the job. You can do a lot of the legwork of employment in a fast, informal fashion by using peer networks. By using these connections, you also give your prospective employee a factor of comfort, because they will have been 'sold' on your business before you call them. Through peer networks you can also ascertain one of the more important questions about prospective employees . . .

PERSONALITY

If you want to build a team rather than just a collection of individuals, every new person you employ has to be able to fit with three things: the business's culture; the owner's culture; and the other employees. This is almost completely a matter of personality. For all of the machines and psychologists now used to appraise these things, peer-assessment is still the best way of knowing if a certain personality will work for your business.

INTERVIEWS

Eventually you'll have to interview candidates regardless of how you've found them. If you sourced them from online advertising, you'll have more to work out about the person. Even if you've been to a recruitment agency, and they give you a rundown of what the person is like, they may present to you differently. And even candidates sourced from peer networks will need your assessment of personality. You just can't escape interviewing.

Here are some tips from my experience of taking part in thousands of interviews:

- Don't make the mistake of many first-time employers and do most of the talking. Do what I suggest with just about any business issue: ask the question. 'Who are you?' 'What do you bring?' 'How can you help this business?'

- If the across-the-desk format is not giving you any insights, break the ice by getting them to do something with you: 'I'm just going down to get a coffee—would you like one?' 'I just have to check something at the loading dock—come for a walk.'
- Don't be worried about getting the person back for two or three interviews if you need to.

I'm not so keen on social markers such as which footy team they support or what music they listen to. In the end, you want to know what they can do for your business goals and whether their personality is going to support that.

GAUGING EXPERIENCE

Some résumés are just plain confusing, with too much information, too many dates, a total mishmash of former work titles. If you're going through twenty of these, you'll get a headache. Some ways to tease out the real experience and whether it's relevant to your goals are:

- Ask the candidate to talk about the most important skill they have picked up in the last five years. Don't let them refer you back to their CV—make them talk about skills, not job descriptions; ability, not titles.
- Alternatively, ask the candidate to talk about a problem they've encountered and what they did about it.
- Don't allow a candidate to read from a CV or to direct you to it. Throw the CV in the bin and make them communicate with you.

The most important thing about assessing someone's experience is to cross-check it. Call the people the candidate used to work for and have a chat.

WORK ETHIC

If you run a hard-working operation where people are encouraged to go after goals and meet deadlines then you don't need someone who keeps looking at the clock. In general terms, it's better to get a hard-working, enthusiastic person with little experience and train them up than it is to get a disengaged, passive employee with tonnes of experience. The enthused person can be taught and turned into an expert, whereas an expert with a bad attitude is never going to become enthused or hard-working and will be a drag on the rest of the team. Luckily for you, an employer is still allowed to discriminate based on a candidate's work ethic. The thing is, you have to make this call before you employ someone, because in Australia you cannot sack a person for being lazy.

AMBITION

When a small private company employs someone with qualifications and experience, the owner can never offer the mobility, status and remuneration of the large organisations. Neither can they offer the security. So if you're trying to attract someone with talent—say in marketing, finance or sales management—in order to boost your business, then you have to put yourself in their shoes and accept that ambitious people will want an inducement to come to your business.

Traditionally, that inducement will be financial: you can offer them bonuses that are tied to meeting goals quarter by quarter. Or the financial inducement could be in the form of equity: if the sales manager can lift the sales revenue by 20 per cent in two years, they get 5 per cent of the business.

If you don't want to use financial incentives, you might have to offer this person something they could never get at a large organisation. Owner-like responsibilities might be one attraction, or a chance to contribute to strategy, or a more entrepreneurial working week. Who knows: if you have the right person, they might be your joint-venture partner when you expand to other sites. Not all ambitious people want more money.

INVESTING IN TRAINING

Have a look at the business owners who have a worse employment record than others and you are probably looking at someone who does not invest in training.

To offer training to a new employee you don't need to go as far as having the processes and manuals that franchises have. But looking at how famous franchises do it might give you ideas. For instance, McDonald's starts employees on one basic thing and expands them outwards until they can do anything, even run the store. McDonald's founder Ray Kroc once said, 'We've got to have talent. And I'm going to put my money in talent' (aboutmcdonalds.com). These days, McDonald's Hamburger University, in the United States, trains 5000 people each year.

As an employer and business-builder, you have to think about what the employee has to know to do their job; what the employee should also know to cover for other key people; and what you want them to learn, as a development path. If you can commit to these three things—and put them in writing, make them part of the business and find the time to make them happen—then you're running ahead of most other private businesses, developing your staff and engaging them in the business.

Training should always start with the skills and processes required to operate the business, but it should try to encompass 'development': development of people, and development of the business. People like to be improved and to gain more skills or simply feel more useful today than they felt yesterday; and businesses, because they exist in a changing environment, need to react by training people for fresh demand in the market.

Development of people is also a good investment if your company is small but ambitious: in these businesses you can't afford to have all the skills in 'silos' held by single people. If you deliver goods to people, more than one employee needs to have their relevant truck licence; if you maintain the things you sell, you need at least one 'trainee' learning how to fix those machines; if your new law firm specialises in mining licences but is most busy with wills and conveyancing, then you need to ensure that the specialists are also trained in wills and conveyancing.

This all comes back to training and development and, yes, you have to invest in it. Don't see it as a chore—see it as a cost of growth. And make this cliché your motto: 'Training is not an event, it's a process.'

BEWARE OF HYPOCRISY

In building a team, hypocrisy is a fatal flaw, yet so many business owners are hypocritical. What happens is that a business owner gets an employment manual from their industry association which tells them to have weekly 'bull sessions' where employees can have their say without fear of recrimination. Or they're supposed to tell employees that there are no failures, only lessons. You know the kind of thing.

Yet when the owner gets defensive about criticism at the weekly session or a mistake earns an employee a screaming tirade from the employer, all of the positive psychological techniques fall in a heap. It only takes a couple of instances where the rhetoric is not met by the reality and you're back to a bunch of employees rather than a team—and a bunch of employees who are disengaged, at best.

My advice is to stay away from faddish tricks such as mission statements, bull sessions, social engagement programs and openness policies unless you actually believe in them.

WHEN IT DOESN'T WORK

Like many employers, I started out trying to be understanding and 'fair' about employees who were not really pulling their weight or whose work ethics didn't get close to mine. But when you expect a certain standard of work from most of your people, but you make an exception for one or two slackers, you are not being 'fair' at all. In fact, you are undermining the workplace culture and confusing the employees who are working very hard for you and your business. So this is what I do nowadays: if someone is not engaged, not interested and not working very hard, I cull them. There are pleasant ways of doing it and there are processes to be adhered to. But when you're the business owner, this is what you do. Letting someone go does not have to be a harsh judgement of them or their character. You may be doing them a favour.

This is not an unusual outlook. Jack Welsh, the former chief executive of GE Corporation, had a 'ten per cent rule'. The ten per cent rule meant that at the end of each year he would identify the bottom ten per cent performers in their respective divisions and he would show them the door. His reasoning wasn't only that a bottom echelon of people is a drag on earnings, but that disengaged people attempt to make those around them disengaged also, and that when you have ten per cent of your work force underperforming, you're excluding all those potential employees who would love to enter your organisation and give you their best effort. It's unlikely that you'd build a small business into a vast corporation within your lifetime, but it's worth thinking about why you want to carry employees who are disengaged, lazy and losing you business with their bad attitude. Always remember that employees are costs to the business; the business employs them, not you. If they're not contributing to earnings in some way, you can not carry them.

•

Just remember, you're the boss, and it's your job to build and motivate the team. If you can't do this totally with imported ideas and imported experts, you'll have to come up with some ideas and systems of your own.

Employing the right people does not always go according to plan. Nine successes out of ten is considered very good going, and when you talk with other business owners you'll find that no one has a 100 per cent strike rate. However, beyond the employment of individuals is the building of teams.

Most people reading this will not be forming divisions or creating layers of bureaucracy to stand over. Most private companies will have little separation between the owner and the most junior employee. So the idea of a team—a little contrived in the corporate or government sectors—is quite real in private businesses. People have responsibilities that overlap one another's; they sit closer; meetings are a blend of executive, management and workers; the successes and failures are felt immediately and equally by all the team (you don't read about your workplace in the newspapers); and decisions are quickly implemented and just as quickly stopped if they're not working.

The smaller your team the more they impact on your business fortunes, which makes the quality of the people in them crucial to your business fortunes. So aside from being careful about who you employ to be part of the team, there's an ongoing job of running a team, not simply as a chore but as an instrument of achieving your goals. This brings us to the subject of leadership.

CHAPTER 16

LEADERSHIP

Teams need leaders. But where do leaders come from?

Some people going into business will have experience as managers, often at senior levels. But this doesn't always translate well to leading a business. Most managers who have done well in a large organisation have not been pure leaders: they have managed their own fortunes between those below and those above them. They are as much an employee as the people they manage. In their corporate lives they've had distinct job descriptions, with discrete duties and responsibilities, and these have been as clearly outlined for them by their superiors as they then have to enforce to their own teams.

Other business owners have not been managers but have been 'stars' of their respective industries: high-profile stockbrokers, bankers, accountants, lawyers, chefs, venture capitalists, builders and sales people all move on from their employed lives and into a business ownership situation. They don't always warm to the role of leading because they haven't been forced to do it before: they've had all had the luxury of turning up, doing their job very well and then being able to go home and forget about it. Others have risen to being middle managers, and have taken voluntary redundancy and are pursuing a dream of being self-employed.

These three main types of employee may have excelled at their roles, earned great bonuses, and been very smart and respected. But they struggle in their own business. Why? Because management isn't leadership, and an executive is not an owner, no matter how distinguished.

THIS IS THE JOB

Running a business has unique stresses and concerns, largely because you're not only asking yourself to be a master of many disciplines, but because your own wealth rides on the outcome of your mastery of these disciplines. Typically, you are the general manager, the public office holder, the company secretary, the responsible entity (for tax purposes), the chief financial officer, the marketing guru, the sales manager, the face of the business, the business's lender of last resort, the paymaster, the workers compensation insurer and the debt collector.

In other words, when you own a business, you are consumed with things that have to be done: things for the bank, things for the government, things for the tax office, things for clients, suppliers and employees. It all falls to you. There is no other person to turn to, most of the time, and so whether you like it or not, you are the leader.

You're the owner—this is the job.

MAKE YOUR TEAM WORK

While the demands of your time and mental energy will be sorely tested in the first two years of owning a business—and in all subsequent growth phases—there is a way through, which can also be an accelerant to growth. That way is to build a good team of people who don't just pick up the duties that you would otherwise be doing yourself, but who eventually become one of the drivers of business growth and therefore your wealth. This happens in layers, and while I have spoken about some of the selection criteria for hiring employees, there is also a functional layering of employment. Here's how it works.

COVERING FOR YOU

One of the first employees most businesses put on is the person who duplicates the technical ability of the owner/founder. If you want to make surfboards, you need someone besides yourself who can do that so you can concentrate on business development and selling the boards. If you want to open a mortgage broker firm, you need someone writing mortgages while you're developing clients.

This replacement or duplication role of employing is a well-established pathway and is usually the first hire you make, because as the owner you realise that your attentions are needed to work *on* the business while someone else is working *in* the business. You hear business people say that they regret going into their chosen field because they don't get to do it anymore. This goes for chefs who have to give up being in the kitchen, and lawyers who only take a few big cases, and shipbuilders who spend most of their time on the phone or working on tender documents.

Duplication is the hire that you are most qualified to do. You know exactly what to look for because you are finding a replacement for yourself. In many businesses, the owner can hire four or five people who duplicate their abilities, until having to employ someone different.

BUILDING A CORE

The next wave of employees will not be achieved by every business owner. It is usually a financial controller or accounts person, followed by either a head of operations or a sales manager. This means that having covered your own expertise, you hire the risk person, the making person and the growth person. With you as the CEO—and people in place to duplicate your technical expertise—a CFO, sales manager and operations chief now form your core. You may call them by different names, and they may do other jobs besides their main function: the finance people often take over the company secretary duties; the operations chief will also oversee the office and IT; and the sales manager often looks after marketing, websites and business development.

In this phase, you are still across everything and are still incredibly busy. But now you have a core of important employees who can ensure three core requirements of your business: that you comply with government, that you can make your goods and services, and that you are selling them. Take your time sourcing and hiring these people—they'll eventually become the management layer and you'll have to rely on them.

SCALE UP

The next phase is the one that most business owners never move to. It is the point at which, having established a core of administration, production and sales people, you move to a level of employees who are growth-drivers, not simply an added cost. This is where their productive output begins to outstrip their wages, creating revenues greater than what was spent to produce the revenues. When you spend on business infrastructure (floor space, machines) in order to expand volume, these employees are the essential ingredient you add so you can realise the profits to be made from the expanded capacity.

In our café example, this is the point where—in order to double the sale of coffees and cookies—several new staff have been employed to service the volumes produced by the extra chairs, the longer hours and perhaps the competitive advantage of the only Timorese organic coffee beans in the neighbourhood. Let's say you and two employees can take $5000 in revenues per five-day week, at the cost of $3000 in three wages. Very simply, doubling the sales may not mean doubling the wages. In order to make $10 000 in revenues per week, it might require one-and-half extra people. So for $4500 in wages, you produce $10 000 in revenues, a significant increase in net profit margin. This is because capacity is always slightly behind or slightly in front of demand. If you invest in a cook when the café first starts and she's only cooking 200 meals per week, you may only require a part-timer to work at peak periods in order to double the sales. It's the same with the coffee side: doubling the coffees from 500 to 1000 per week may only require one extra person: so now you have one on the coffee machine, one at the till (you) and one serving tables.

BE A LEADER

There's just one catch to building a team: these are not machines or computers. They are people and they have to be managed, guided and motivated. And only one person can do it—you.

A leader is different to a manager in that the leader has to be followed rather than obeyed. In this respect, when you own a company the example you set for the employees will be worth more than anything else. When deciding how this is going to happen, just remember that regardless of how stressful your own concerns are, you are the main authority figure for most of the people you employ. Even if there's only two or three or five of them, you're the boss for 40 hours of the week. And when you lay down rules or ask for behavioural standards, you're creating a culture every bit as strong as any institution's.

So, if you have this power, have a think about how you'll use it. How will you lead? Will you insist on good manners, no swearing and a positive, can-do attitude? If this is your culture, you'd better start living it. In my businesses, employees know that dishonesty is the break-point for me. I have zero tolerance for liars, and the people I employ and partner with understand this. What are your benchmarks for behaviour? People follow leaders, so you should instil good habits in the place rather than bad, because setting a culture is a chance to ensure that the business reflects what's important to you. If you want the employees to be punctual and take deadlines seriously, then you have to get on the floor and work with them occasionally, show them that these things are important. If focusing on goals and driving hard to achieve them is part of the business image you want to build, then instil it by being it. I do this in my businesses: being curious about the market and restless about improvement is something that drives me, and for me this is expressed in continuous questioning. I question our assumptions, our marketing, our branding, our handling of deals and our financial statements. I do this in every meeting and every email and every presentation. I believe a constant round of questions about your business is a good way to keep it fine-tuned in a dynamic market, and I want employees and branch managers to do the same thing. But I don't put posters in the staff kitchen to tell people to be more curious, more challenging of the market assumptions they are reacting to. I don't think leaders can form a culture by doing this. I think you have to form the culture based on what you find important, and acting in a way that demonstrates that it's important.

I talk to many people who never thought much about leadership until they became an employer. They usually go looking for leadership ideas in books and seminars. But, actually, if you have the wherewithal to start a business and grow it, you have all the leadership skills already inside you. I don't believe you need fancy speeches or mission statements pinned to the kitchenette wall:

you need to project what's important to you, every day of the week, and show that these values create success for the business. If you do this in a positive, inclusive way, you will gain followers and set a corporate culture that's hard to break.

Me? Every Friday I text or email or call every one of the 140 Yellow Brick Road franchisees around Australia. I talk about sales, talk about new products, point out news in the *Australian Financial Review* that affects us; I thank them for the week and ask them to get back to me with their concerns and questions. Which they do. Once a month I travel around Australia for a few days seeing as many branch mangers as I can, talking about issues, hearing feedback about ad campaigns and new financial products.

Some people see this as intrusive or nosey. It isn't—it's a statement about what I find important, which is communicating successes and difficulties, and relying on your team-mates, even if we're in Sydney and they're in Mt Isa. This part of what I do is leadership, not management. It isn't contrived or scripted. It's what's important to me, and therefore to my business. It's what you do when you're the leader.

GOOD MANAGERS

Being an employer isn't all about leadership. If it was, we wouldn't need managers. It's just that when you're a business owner you do a lot of managing along with the leading, and how you do this has a big impact on how well the business performs, what kind of clients you attract and whether you retain staff.

Being a good manager, I believe, is as much an art as a science. However there are a few basics that everyone can learn.

HIRE WELL

I mentioned this earlier. Decide who you want in the business, on a personality basis, and aim for them. It's easier to teach an enthusiastic, honest person how to do something new than it is to get a work ethic out of a lazy expert. If you can't stand lazy, clock-watching people, don't hire them.

HAVE CLEAR EXPECTATIONS

If you're lucky enough to have attracted self-starting people to your business, then you get to avoid the instructional method of dealing with employees, and you can instead concentrate on what's expected. For people who know how to take responsibility, communicating expectations is far more powerful than issuing instructions twenty times a day. Be clear about your expectations and these people will respond.

COMMUNICATE

Without exception, the best managers I have seen have been good communicators. They are direct, forceful when they have to be, well mannered and also good listeners. If you want to be a good manager, you could do worse than starting at this point. Good managers use certain techniques to emphasise their communications. One is to use positive language, even when complaining about something. Another is to ask the question rather than make the accusation. Or talk about outcomes rather than process. Most of all, good communicators think about what they're going to say before they say it, and they never talk to someone in a way they wouldn't like to be spoken to themselves.

EMPOWER

Good managers find a way to empower workers by getting them to use initiative and creativity, make decisions and work to goals rather than orders. If you get a critical mass of employees feeling empowered, you will build quickly.

ALIGNMENT

I referred to this earlier in the book and it is a powerful management tool. The ability to bring the interests of the employee closer to those of the business owner can produce the extra 5 or 10 per cent of effort or output that can change many things for your business. This means having to construct a bonus system, which I have always felt should be spread around the team rather than tailored to an individual. However you do it, aligning workers with the owner is a good way of motivating people and retaining them.

UPSKILLING

In all of my businesses I have endeavoured to make professional education and development a perk that everyone enjoys. You may not have the budget to offer this, but you can do something just as good: insist that every employee is trained for the job above or beside them. People like to learn new skills and they like to feel they can step up to their superior's chair, when the day comes. It is a motivating policy and one that creates loyalty.

DON'T HAVE FAVOURITES

A fast way to break up a team effort and make people fight one another is to be a manager who has a favourite. It can be hard not to favour a person who's doing a particularly good job or who's driving growth in a part of the business that you're keen to pursue. But having a teacher's pet—while nice for your ego—is destructive to the team. So don't play favourites, be a mentor.

MENTORING

Most owners are so busy that mentoring is one of the things that drops off their weekly to-do list. That's a pity, because mentoring is a valuable way of retaining good staff, lifting up the underperformers and building a team. Mentoring is often written about in either technical terms or 'new age' jargon. That is, it's either reduced to structured programs or it's almost psychotherapy.

The most effective mentoring, I believe, is the kind where the best qualities are encouraged out of a person as a counterpoint to the burdens of performance that inform their daily routine. This means building a relationship with an employee, showing patience and humour, and getting them to challenge themselves with questions.

Mentoring is really a desire to develop the *person* rather than supercharge the employee. As such, many employees will be resentful if they feel you're reading from a manual you bought from an HR company. If you're going to invest time and effort in developing a person in your business, do it from your heart.

REMUNERATION

Part of your management duties—as opposed to leadership—will be to ensure that all employees are remunerated appropriately. Generally, this process will be a balance between three forces: industry norms, benchmarks being met, and general pay rises in your workplace. I suggest you run a sub-file on each employee, entitled 'remuneration', where you note conversations and reminders on what was discussed. I don't believe you have to make annual remuneration changes. What's required is scheduled performance reviews and an interview. And a small tip: sometimes you have to offer a pay rise before you're asked. If you ask someone to step up and take on more responsibility, you have to reward them if they succeed.

THE ROLE OF THE OWNER

When it comes to attracting the right people into your business, you may be at a loss to explain to yourself why they would do it. Many business owners have trodden this path. They have had to ask themselves: 'Why would this senior person at a major publishing house come and work for me in my start-up publishing business?' or 'What could I offer the marketing guru at a major corporation to come and work for me in this small firm I've just started?'

These questions are always the most vexing in the boom industries. If you're building a diesel maintenance firm, how do you compete with West Australian mining companies who are paying a diesel mechanic twice what you can offer? If a civil engineer is doing big projects with a big company, how do you attract that person away from their secure lifestyle?

The answer, really, is to look at what makes you unique, rather than what makes you the underdog. The thing about you is that you're the owner. You have agility, you have upside, you have the capacity to make decisions and to let senior people join you in major decisions. Many smart and ambitious people will be interested in this if they feel they've gone far enough in a large company. But mostly, you own the shares and you have the owner's equity in the business. This gives you the capacity to attract high quality people with a stake in the fortunes of the business. That is, you allow selected people to own some of the business equity and to be rewarded annually when the dividends are paid. How you structure this is a matter to be discussed with your accountants.

Never count yourself out of the race for top talent just because your business is small. If you can show a pipeline of work or potential work, and you have strong owner's equity, you're at least in with a chance of attracting very good people. Of course, you have to accept that your equity is a source of remuneration—something many business owners find hard to give away.

THE SMART OPERATOR

The ongoing battles of doing business will take in parts of you that are the leader, the manager and the owner. But the person seen most often is the operator, the person on the ground making decisions, talking to banks, negotiating with suppliers, cutting deals, making compromises, diverting employees, altering plans, resolving conflicts, making allies and banking the cheques. We don't talk much about entrepreneurs in the business world: we talk about 'good operators', 'smart operators'.

The smart operator has employees to increase their sales and revenues, but they may spend more of their time managing the myriad of people and organisations who have to be dealt with. These people may not be employees, as such, but they supply crucial services and goods that have to be paid for. Accordingly, even if they're not employed by you, they still work for you and they need leadership and management as much as any employee, and sometimes more: those outside the culture you're building—no matter how well known their brand—may do things slightly differently and you have to keep watch over what they're doing.

These contractors and advisers will be particularly prevalent when you are expanding your business or moving to a new site. They include lawyers, accountants, bankers, finance brokers, insurance brokers, real estate agents, marketing experts, PR firms, couriers, temping agencies, freight companies, IT consultants, cabling firms, phone companies, stationery suppliers and rubbish contractors.

As with any employment situation—whether they are full-time employees, contractors or suppliers—you have to manage external providers. The most common way to do this is to start with whether you need them: Before going to the lawyers, do you have internal skills for basic legals? Rather than hiring couriers, do you have delivery people doing runs around the city anyway? If you need to hire experts, how much value do they bring? Do they simply do something no one else can do? Do they help you comply with regulations and laws? Or do they create more income for your business?

It's worth knowing which box they fit into because that should help you form an opinion about how much you should be paying them and whether they are worth it. 'Worth', in this case, can be decided in three ways:

- Does the external provider deliver what they promise and solve a problem?
- Does the external provider respond to detailed requests?
- Does the external provider cost more than the value created?

CHAPTER 17

TOWARDS AN EXIT

The reason that your goal has to live at the beginning of your business planning is that it must inform what you do every day. Your actions revolve around KPIs, which build to the main benchmark of EBIT earnings: that is, earnings before interest and tax.

Let's examine again what the goal was: to sell the business for twice the price you bought it for. Cafés are valued at an average earnings multiple of 2 ×. This means a buyer will take net earnings of your café—possibly averaged over two years—and simply double the figure. And that figure is the starting point of the negotiation that will lead to a sale price.

Since the day you opened for business, you have been focused on how to raise the earnings figure of this business from $100 000 per annum to $200 000. This figure is the profitability of the business because it is the annual revenue minus the operating expenses (before interest and taxation). Your goal is to double the earnings of the business in five years or less, and thereby have the business valued for sale at $400 000. This will give you a capital gain of $200 000, but also be mindful of the salary you paid yourself during your ownership. The $200 000 is a bonus payment, since you were earning a salary the whole time.

GROWING SALES

As I have canvassed in the planning chapters, the main focus for you is raising sales revenues, while keeping costs low, or at the very least, not allowing costs to increase at the same pace as sales.

In a simple business such as a café, the sales increase can be done by:

- Expanding the number of seats that the café has, thereby expanding the capacity to hold customers.
- Extending the hours of the café, thereby expanding the capacity of the business to sell beverages, snacks and meals.
- Introducing a competitive advantage, such as rare Timorese organic coffee, which draws in extra customers and can be sold at a higher margin per cup than normal coffee.
- Promoting your expertise with coffee making, coffee selection, etc.
- Promoting that the café is under new management.
- Expanding the capacity of coffee making, cookie storage and the kitchen to create the ability to meet increased sales volumes.
- Hiring extra staff to ensure extra volume doesn't slow service.
- Creating a loyalty card system to drive sales growth.

- Advertising in local media, social media or with 'get one free' vouchers.
- Installing new décor, with a theme as cool as the surrounding neighbourhood.

Whether you do all this at once, with a loan from the bank or whether you do it incrementally—funded from café cash flow—generally speaking a new owner has to make an investment in the business assets in order to lift sales from where they were at purchase to where you want to take them.

The above example of what can be done to increase sales in a café can be pushed to most businesses as generic sales-building ideas:

- expand capacity
- increase staff
- advertise
- promote a competitive advantage or novel feature
- promote the firm's expertise
- match your décor to who you want to attract
- promote the fact that the business is under new management.

Let's say you borrow $50 000 to make your improvements at the café: as soon as the expanded capacity and marketing has begun, you have to get back to focusing on the KPIs you have chosen to observe. In a café, these will be:

- cups of coffee sold per day
- cookies sold per day
- meals sold per day.

Following KPIs should become your obsession. Not to the point of total paranoia, but certainly to the point of being worried. There will be weekly figures that you enter into your spreadsheets to plot your sales revenues growth. But it's the daily counting that tells you about the market. If your Thursdays are weak, why? Can you work that out? Do you know who's not turning up on Thursdays? If you can target this group on Thursdays with a campaign (half-price Thursdays), you might add 50 cups, 50 cookies and twenty meals per week to your count. That may only add $500 to your sales revenue for the week, but it helps cover the fixed overheads of staff and rent and brings sales back to the business.

Which is the name of the game, remember—doubling the earnings.

The changing of hours is something that you can try for a set amount of time, to see what happens to sales. In most industries you find that 80 per cent of the businesses fill 20 per cent of the available time. They congregate around opening times (think banks, pubs, fish and chip shops). Most cafés in major cities and regional centres would open at around 7.30 a.m. If you look around your rivals in the neighbourhood and find that the earliest opener is 7.30, you have an opportunity: become the earliest by opening at 6.30 a.m. This may not trigger a flood of café-goers to begin with, but it gives you a competitive advantage to capture all those tradies and morning dog-walkers who would otherwise be going to McDonald's. Think it through further. What do tradies want along with their coffee at 6.30 a.m.? They want something they can eat in the ute. So why not come up with a 'combo' product of coffee and bacon-and-egg roll for $7? Morning walkers may want a place to tie up the dog and a bowl of water for it, or they might want to browse the day's newspapers with their coffee.

If this works, and your daily sales count starts rising, you're on your way. The point of the exercise is to find the competitive advantage not by reinventing the wheel but by adapting to what the market wants. Remember my initial points about opening a business: a business is simply an entity that supplies goods and services to meet aggregate demand. The market is the price that is struck for the goods and services. In all of my businesses, finding a way to meet aggregate demand has been the key to success, and that process starts with polling what the demand actually *is*, as opposed to what the incumbents have decided *should* be the demand. In my first big financial services business—Wizard Home Loans—the initial idea was to differentiate ourselves by creating mobile lenders who would go to the borrower. This, along with a call centre and a website application portal, was going to make it easier for Australians to get a mortgage and also lower our unit costs, thereby allowing us to market mortgages at a lower interest rate than the major banks. There was one small problem: our early feedback showed that while Australians in the regions loved our brand and our products and our costs, they wanted a branch to walk into. They wanted to talk to someone.

Oops! We quickly acted on what we were being told and built a branch network through Australia and New Zealand that eventually numbered more than 230 branches. We listened to the market and we acted. It turned out that Australians didn't want to turn their backs on the banks: they wanted a service and a personal interaction—at a branch—that felt the same as banks *used* to be. It's just that no one had asked them. The lesson here can be used by all businesses trying to find a competitive advantage or a niche in an existing market: you don't have to reinvent the wheel in line with what you believe the customers should want; all you have to do is ask them and, if you can, meet their demand. In every single industry there's an incumbent group of firms who have established the standard offering to the market, and it's usually an offering that suits the incumbents—this applies to Telstra and ANZ Bank as much as it does to the hair salons and greengrocers in your local high street. Your job, as a business owner who is focused on growth in line with an exit strategy, is to establish what the market really wants, and then find a way to deliver it in a profitable way.

SHRINKING COSTS

Of course, the 'earnings' you are aiming for are expressed as revenues-less-operating expenses. And so while you are focused on increasing capacity, driving customer volumes and sales, you must also be focused on controlling operating expenses—the cost of doing business. This is not easy in a growth phase because the very time when costs are likely to increase is when you're growing.

So your job is to find a way to keep them as low as possible without hindering your ability to grow revenues. Some of your costs will be fixed, such as your lease and the interest payments on your business loan. Others, such as employees, will become fixed when you settle on staffing levels. Costs can also fluctuate, with weather (power bill), sales (food bill), growth strategy (marketing costs) and the global price of commodities (coffee and sugar).

There's usually some cost savings in a business, especially a business you've bought from another owner. Some ideas for possible cost savings include:

- Running staffing levels that correspond to revenues (don't overstaff).
- Hiring hard-working people who know what they're doing.
- Being vigilant about basic supplies and always asking about cheaper alternatives.
- Investigating discounts for buying in greater bulk.
- Challenging the landlord for rent reductions if there are faults in the premises.
- Refining your ordering to eliminate waste and spoilage.
- Reviewing your phone package—do you need a landline, for instance?
- Reviewing your data package—do you really need the 100GB deal?
- Asking an insurance broker to review your insurances.

Costs should be followed and treated with their own KPIs. And rather than treating them as the poorer cousin to sales, think about cost savings as earnings. If you can shave $500 a week off your overheads by changing your ordering or baking your own muffins, then your earnings figure just jumped by $500. It doesn't matter where it came from—in fact, a structural change that saves $500 per week is probably more permanent than a spike in sales.

While the main KPI for reaching your goal is going to be sales revenues, your secondary KPIs should be around costs: Where are they greatest? Can they be reduced? At what point of cost-saving is sales growth affected?

All of these need work by you. You need a pad and pen and a spreadsheet in your laptop and you need to start measuring costs growth against sales revenue growth. The two lines should diverge, with sales revenue growing faster than costs. This is when you're finding scale, growing your earnings and getting close to the goal of doubling them.

While this trade-off between revenues and costs is fought on a broad scale, there are more pointed KPIs that can be done to test the profitability of every sale. Business advisers and accountants can set up the systems to do this, but you can try it yourself. You simply factor in all the revenues from one line—say, cups of coffee—and divide them by the number of units sold in a week. Take the revenues from coffees as a percentage of the whole and apply that to the fixed overheads of the business. Subtract the coffee bean costs and the wages of the barista. You won't find a way to track the profitability of your coffee in one day. It might take a couple of weeks, but once you have it, you can build your own metrics for how much you make per cup of coffee, then how much extra you make if they also buy a cookie. Once you have this down, you can even see how the unit profitability changes by the hour of the day, by the day itself and by the weather.

Running KPIs on your costs, down to this level of detail, is not obsessive or strange. It is the basis of all business—if you can understand your costs properly then you can ensure profits from the growing sales you're making. If you don't understand your costs down to profitability per sale then you're always slightly blind in how you push forward. There are many businesses that chase sales growth without making a science of the corresponding costs, and they pay the price in poor earnings figures, low owner's equity and, sometimes, insolvency. One of the most damaging things you can do is push forward with sales growth when each sale is losing you money. In fact, the growth phase is the time when a small business is most likely to go out of business.

It sounds a little tedious, and those from a non-financial background may think that this kind of measurement is not what they're about. But it works. Remember this motto: if you can measure it, you can manage it.

GOOD PRICES

The race towards an exit brings many formerly blurry parts of the business puzzle into focus. As you get going and really focus on the earnings multiple, there arises the practical question of where your earnings growth is going to come from. While sales and costs are the foremost KPIs you'll look at, there are other ways. Once you get down to profit margin per unit, you realise something else: you don't only boost the margin by reducing costs, you can also do it by charging more. This works two ways: price and value.

Let's start with price. As I have warned elsewhere in this book, be very, very careful of a strategy—in any industry—where you seek to claw back your purchase cost and build earnings by raising your prices.

This is a common scenario among people who are either desperate or inexperienced. It is why most good franchises have an absolute rule about what the retail price of each item will be. And it is why the car companies attempt to control what prices their dealers put on new vehicles. The reason is simple: in a competitive economy, the market is the point at which supply meets demand and a price is set. The market is all of us deciding what price to pay. When a single player breaks from the pack and raises their price, it is almost as certain as night following day that their sales will start to drop. The only difference in the story from here on in will be how fast the sales drop and how quickly the owner realises their mistake and reverses course. The negative effects of a price strategy can be quite dramatic with commodity items such as cars, grocery items and, yes, coffee.

The typical scenario is that the customers will slowly drift away from your expensive coffee to what they serve next door, which is the same thing but 50 cents cheaper. None of this will surprise any reader, yet right now—somewhere in Australia—a business owner who sells what everyone else sells is contemplating pricing themselves out of the market. They will do it, their sales will fall, their earnings—after a short spike—will fall, their owner's equity will erode and they will have to sell their business at a low price based on the earnings multiple (which is where they came in with their purchase of that distressed café).

So be very careful with price, whether you are building a courier business, a fencing company, a law firm or a laundromat. And remember this: on readily available products, the market decides price, not the business owner. This situation—which the majority of business owners operate under—is called being a 'price taker'. That is, you don't have much control—if any—over what you can charge for your goods or services. In the case of a café owner, coffee is a global commodity and you have to pay the going price for it, and unless you have a monopoly location with no alternatives, you are heavily constrained in what you charge for a coffee because everyone knows what they should be paying. The only time this rule changes is when you have a complete monopoly due to location (the customer has no choice) or the market is controlled by a few incumbents, in which case the price is controlled by the ensuing oligopoly.

The exception to the rule is when you find the competitive advantage or the novel feature. In your café, this could be the organic Timorese coffee beans, fresh-baked muffins or a dog-friendly area. Even then you have to be careful with how you market the product in order to justify the higher prices.

Value for Money

Price is dangerous, but value can drive profitable sales if you hit the right note. In a café, for instance, you might extend your hours into the evening and introduce full meals. A properly costed meal produces excellent margins because you are selling something for more money but providing the value. You could do a similar thing in the mornings by introducing homemade muesli; it can be made for 60 cents but sold for $4 a bowl. People will buy it because they perceive the value and, besides, some people just like muesli in the mornings.

This rule runs across all industries: value can win where price has failed. Bus companies will pay 20 per cent more for a Mercedes-Benz bus because it will last for twenty years, while the competition lasts less than ten. Caterpillar is the most expensive earthmoving machinery you can buy, yet this company dominates the global mining business. Why? It lasts.

•

In the businesses I have run, there have been people more suited to cutting costs and those who are better at making sales and developing business opportunities. But when you start a business, you have to make yourself be both: the costs hawk and the growth guru. Your main goal is an earnings figure of $200 000, which is revenues after you take away the operating expenses. Whether you focus on the cost savings or the sales growth, both have to be healthy if you are going to reach an earnings target that delivers your goal.

This is not as hard as it sounds. Just always remember that costs savings boost your earnings, so cutting costs is the same as a big sale. Live by the motto: a penny saved is a penny earned.

CHAPTER 18

GETTING OUT

As you drive sales, cut costs and increase your earnings, you move closer to your exit and valuation of the business. If you have moved your KPIs in the direction they were supposed to go and you have the earnings to prove it, after a few years choices will open up and you will have to make decisions in two broad categories. These are:

- choice of exit
- earnings or equity.

THE LOW-DOWN ON EQUITY

I want to start with the second issue because, while I have alluded to the different ways of exiting your business, I have so far kept away from exploring the potential of owner's equity and what it can mean for your sale options. There are good reasons for this. One of them is that when building a business around a sale price, you have to be aiming for one valuation model. It's hard to have two goals simultaneously, and the earnings multiple model is one that is simple for business owners to understand. It also has the advantage of being publicly listed by organisations such as the Australian Society of CPAs and BizExchange, so you can read the historic 'high' and 'low' multiples paid for businesses in certain industries.

Firstly, the differences between earnings and equity. Earnings are one way the *market* values your business. It simply lands on a revenues-minus-operating expenses figure and multiplies it by the industry earnings multiple to give an indicative value to the business. So the earnings multiple is a relationship between the market and your business.

Equity is a relationship between *you* and your business. It does not rely on the market measurements of revenues and earnings, rather it relies on an accounting principle of ALE, or Assets + Liabilities = Equity.

So, let's say the assets of your café are $200 000 and the liabilities (including the $50 000 bank loan) are $150 000. With no other complications, you having owner's equity of $50 000. It is worth noting that the liabilities in the above scenario include the $100 000 that you put into the business. As unfair as it sounds, this seed capital is treated by the accounting profession as a liability to the business because it is capital that must be returned to the owner.

Equity is traditionally bracketed with debt, because all companies carry both, and one always rises as the other reduces. So, as your café pays back the $100 000 capital, its liabilities reduce and your equity rises.

I've put this discussion on equity and earnings into this chapter on exits because owner's equity can drive different but lucrative exits for the business owner. Before talking about this, it's worth noting that in the business world there are definitely owners who focus on earnings multiples and owners who are very protective about their equity. Earnings-driven people are usually mindful of their business value being a market matter, whereas equity owners see their equity as something created by sweat and pain, and they jealously guard it. Some, like me, are focused on both.

As you can judge, business owners who build a solid enterprise over a number of years can develop a lot of equity. Their rising equity over the years has meant that banks will lend to them, and they use this borrowing power to buy business land and premises, further developing their wealth. This gives them different options for exiting, which include:

- **Management buy-out (MBO)**—Let's say you develop an engineering business that corners a niche in construction cranes. You have a good run, build a staff of 50 employees and build cranes for companies all over Australia. You have equity of $3 million in the business, which runs low debt levels and produces cranes at a premium price. At the same time, your annual 'earnings' are only $400 000, because you run a high-overheads enterprise and you've been hit by power prices. How do you realise the value of your equity, which is obviously much higher than value based on an earnings multiple? What many cashing-out owners do is allow their management team to buy out their equity and take over the business. The owner receives $3 million and the business has new owners who know the business.

- **Spreading ownership**—Business owners don't always want to walk away from the business. The owner of the crane engineering business could also sell a portion of his shares to employees—making it more affordable to them—and still earn dividend income off the business as a silent equity partner. Owners who want to retire can be attracted to using their equity in this way: they get a lump sum and regular dividend income.

- **Purchase**—Owner's equity can also be used to make acquisitions in preparation for a sale. The equity in the engineering firm can be used to buy another similar business with high earnings. The engineering firm then sells the combined entity for the combined earnings multiple, creating a significant sale price. But the entire deal was only made possible by leveraging the equity in the first business.

- **Generational handover**—When a family business is being passed on to a next generation, equity and debt can be juggled to pay out the owner, compensate the siblings who aren't going into the business, and leave a debt–equity mix in the business for the incoming new generation owner.

- **Initial public offering (IPO)**—Solid equity can attract a venture capitalist to the right business in the right industry, with the right competitive advantage (technology or process, usually). The venture capitalist buys around 30 per cent of the equity and works with the owner—as well as imported experts—to build the company for public listing. Everyone shares in the windfall when it lists.

Most important for business owners who have strong equity in their business is the borrowing power that comes with it. Banks lend against business equity, especially when assets include property, plant and premises. This is quite aside from the performance metrics such as sales, earnings and margins. When a business is a lean, well-run enterprise with low debt and high owner's equity, the options go beyond building sales and accepting an earnings multiple as the sale price. Owners—rather than selling—can borrow against their equity, buy another business, install management in their first one, and roll out their improvement strategies to the new business. Or they don't have to borrow: they can take on a partner who buys some of their equity, and use that as either their cash-out money or the stake to buy another business.

EXIT ROUTES

You started this journey with a goal of doubling earnings to $200 000 and selling the café for a 2 × earnings multiple, or $400 000. You've developed the sales, cut the costs and pushed the annual earnings to where they have to be. Now you have to get the money. How will you do this?

As I've mentioned earlier, there are accepted ways to sell your business. These include:

- **Trade sale**—Your business is listed for sale on a business exchange or via the solicitor-accountant networks. Your intermediary—solicitor, accountant, business adviser, business broker—screens calls and develops a list. The price is usually negotiated around an earnings multiple.
- **Distressed sale**—If your business has drifted towards insolvency, it could go into administration (by creditors), voluntary administration (by you) or be liquidated (by court order). Either way, a registered accountant sells as much of the business for the highest return—often through auction and tender—and then pays off the creditors (and himself) and hands on the remainder to you.
- **Merger**—Another business owner may approach you with the idea of a merger. This happens when you have complimentary niches or overlapping specialities, and joining could reduce costs and raise sales. Your business is 'sold' into a new entity, creating dividends for you if you wish to take them.
- **Acquisition**—Perhaps, when the time comes to exit, another business steps up to attempt to buy you. This often happens when a business decides to buy scale, or when a business in one city wants to expand into another.
- **Partial buy-out**—Let's say there are three shareholders in your café. You may sell your shares to the other shareholders, which means you exit the business. Whether you strike an earnings multiple valuation of the business, or you value your equity, will depend on the shareholders' document that formed the business.
- **Initial public offering**—Lastly, you could issue public offer shares through the Australian Stock Exchange and become a

'public' company. This is an exit because the people who held the shares in the private entity are selling their shares in the new entity to the public.

These are the methods of making your exit, but in reality most private business owners will exit via a trade sale or an acquisition. (The other popular way, a partial buy-out from other shareholders, is an equity transaction as described above.) The accepted way to sell by acquisition or trade sale is through an earnings multiple. But these things don't just happen. In order to get the best sale price for your business, there are a number of issues you have to focus on.

LEAD TIME

All business sales require a decent lead time between the decision to sell and the sale itself. There are many aspects of the business to be tidied up, not unlike the list of repairs and improvements that you get from a real estate agent when you want to sell a house. These things take time when you're talking about a business, and in particular, the accountants and solicitors acting for the purchaser will ask for at least one or two years worth of books and tax returns. So give yourself more than a year to prepare.

ADVISERS

Your leading advisers in a business sale are generally your account-ants and your solicitors. Most mid-sized firms of accountants and solicitors specialise in business sale and purchase, since private business is the rump of their client lists. In any case, I would assume that you have already used these people in your business growth and now are asking them to prepare you for sale and to help you get your target price. The accountants will typically set a timetable for you, knowing that deadlines are the only way to drive a business sale.

GETTING READY

The accountants will work in your business—or give you KPIs to engineer—in order to shift the books of your business towards supporting the higher range of earnings multiple. If they feel the margins are slack, you'll have a year to work on them. If the staffing is low—and you're paying yourself too little—they'll ask you to rectify this to show that the business doesn't rely too much on the owner's labour. If the lease was short-term, they'll ask you to seek a long-term lease—buyers want certainty of premises. The accountants may want costs controlled or earnings slightly higher. You will have time to work on it.

The solicitors control the acceptance of money from the buyers and shift the title from you to the buyer. This may involve some rearranging of your structure because typically the buyer wants to purchase your business but not the corporate entity (and therefore tax liability) that owns it.

Overall, the accountants are looking to fine-tune a business to resemble what the buyers are looking for: a walk-in, turnkey operation with predictable costs, regular earnings, a competitive advantage or novel feature, and a niche in an industry that is strong. Buyers want to buy earnings, not the struggle to get those earnings. So above all they want to know that the way those earnings are derived is not dependent on the current owner, but is brand-based, systemised, business-centric and able to be conducted by the new owner and staff.

OTHER ADVISERS

Your accountants may want to bring additional advisers into the preparation phase, depending on your business and industry, and how much you want to spend to get your target price. These advisers will have specialist expertise in marketing or logistics or IT: areas where a short, sharp improvement can boost the value of the business.

With larger private businesses, your accountants might want to appoint what they call a 'turnaround guy' to your business for a few months, to make changes to your basic costs structure and systems. It's your call whether to let these people in: the good ones can create an extra 20 or 30 per cent in your sale price.

The key adviser introduced by your accountants will be the business broker. This person creates the feedback about how the business is looking, where the demand is and what buyers are looking for. Business brokers run their own databases of people buying and selling, but they are also in the networks of solicitors and accountants.

ASSETS

Advisers are looking for additional valuation factors and they usually lie in the under-reported and overlooked assets. Loans from the business to owners are assets (although not the kind that a buyer will want); long-term supply arrangements can be assets if they are formatted as contracts (your advisers will want to convert arrangements to contracts); intellectual property is an under-reported asset in private business and good advisers will tease this out, repackage it and find a valuation. For instance, many companies can't afford the big enterprise resource planning (ERP) computer systems that corporations use, so their IT person writes code and develops their own systems. If it works and works well, this is an asset, even if you don't market it to other parties. Technology can also go unreported in a business, yet it might have an asset value. This doesn't have to be a new engine or microprocessor—it can be a process or a system. You may have developed a faster way to clear mortgage applications from your clients; you might have a new process for fixing steel together. It may be an app you developed for the iPhone to help your sales people. Help your advisers with these things—they can all add to the asking price.

INFORMATION MEMORANDA

As the particulars of your business coalesce into a picture that the accountants believe will achieve the desired price, they will start work on a detailed information memorandum that will initially go to the business broker to be input into their systems. This detailed version of your business—covering three years, showing sales growth, revenues growth, profit growth, costs and earnings—will be produced and refined, but held back. A very basic one-pager will be the document that prospective buyers see. When the business broker receives a sufficient amount of interest, the detailed memorandum will be released to parties deemed to be serious about purchase.

SETTING A PRICE

The business broker may have named a sale price in his advertising, or given a range, or simply listed the earnings of your business and asked for expressions of interest. Given that the indicative earnings multiples for cafés (in the sub $500 000 turnover range) ranges from around 1 to 4 ×, there is a large scope for different offers (in the case of your café, from $200 000 to $800 000). Setting the price can start after the first offers come in, and the broker declines (much like an auction). Or, the offers value-up to your expectation of $400 000 and you accept (much like a tender). Most offers in a business sale are conditional: that is, they rely on the buyer conducting due diligence via his advisers. Due diligence can take a week and is a risky task in that it is designed to find the things that are not revealed in your detailed memorandum.

In reality, it is never this smooth. The buyer doesn't want to pay any more for the earnings than he has to, and so due diligence is often a leverage for the buyer to pay less than he first offered. This brings the offer and acceptance process into a negotiation. At this point, it is best to have your accountants run the deal.

ACCEPTING THE OFFER

When you are finally made a binding offer that you accept, the journey is completed . . . for now. The solicitors now step in and arrange the contracts of sales and conveyance, giving you the money and the business to the buyer.

•

This brings you back to the start, back to the goal of doubling your earnings so you could double the money you paid for the business in the first place. This is the idea behind all successful businesses and business people. It's about understanding what the market wants and will pay, and aiming for a position in that market that delivers you a profit. Whether this is reducing your costs per cup of coffee to boost your unit margins, or whether you're trying to double your business earnings so you can double its value, it's all the same: it's about finding growth opportunities and pushing them hard until they deliver in results.

An aggressive growth strategy doesn't have to end in a sale inside of five years. You can take on equity partners and expand the business, opening more branches or offices. You can use your momentum and equity to build a franchising model or you can be acquired by a large entity.

The point of the growth exercise is to use small measures and unit improvements to drive results, and the result is to have the business valued by the market at twice what you bought it. What you decide to do with this value—which will probably mean an increase in your equity if you haven't borrowed too much—is up to you.

As with all market-based business, you are part of a cycle. Having built the business to a point where a newcomer can 'buy a job' and live on the earnings that it makes, you have taken the premium that such a business attracts and you will move on to another business. This is what business-builders do. It's not unlike the private-equity people who operate at a high level, buying and rebuilding a struggling company and then reselling it when the earnings are regular and the costs are under control. Venture capitalists do a similar task in the economy, buying equity from business owners and building the earnings of the business to an exit price.

It shouldn't matter if you want to take this growth journey, or you want a stable suburban small business that pays you a salary: making your business the best it can be is going to suit both goals. Learning the power of goal-setting, strategy and execution are valuable for a business regardless of your ultimate ambitions. After all, a nice home is a nice home, whether you renovated it to live in or you rebuilt it to sell at a profit. The same goes for a business: healthy enterprises deliver financial rewards to the owners whether they are the source of a salary for the owner, or whether they are being groomed for a trade sale or investment from a venture capitalist.

Focus on quality and the rewards will come.

CHAPTER 19

YOUR BUSINESS
AND *YOU*

I have been lucky in my business life to have mentors who helped me adjust to new challenges and show me the way through problems. And as you will understand when you have your own business, it's all a problem.

There are tips and methods I have picked up in my career thus far. Most of them I have shared with you on the technical, business-focused side of things. But there are personal techniques that the business owner—and also ambitious employees—can practise that allow them to stay functioning at an optimum level even when the fatigue, stress and fear threaten to overwhelm them.

These are not typical business issues, although they should be because they will derail a hard-working person as readily as a bad business deal or a wrong move in the corporate sphere.

WHEN *YOU* GET IN THE WAY

Although I emphasise the positive sides of business—focus on growth, set your goals, communicate positively, never be satisfied with second best, and so on—I also accept that many of the things business owners and corporate/professional high-flyers will have to deal with will be negative. Often, when someone asks me about whether they would do well owning a business, I ask them a few personality-centred questions. They include:

- Can you work an eighteen-hour day when required? Can you work in a state of exhaustion for weeks? Can you make yourself get out of bed in the morning, and can you make others do it, too?
- When delayed income and mounting bills come together with staff problems, can you keep it together? When the pressure becomes unbearable, can you keep working?
- Can you look in the mirror, ask 'What am I doing here?', then confidently answer? Do you feel energised by your purpose, and can you make your business reflect the purpose?
- Can you set an example that others want to follow? Can you make others feel as if they can achieve what you want them to achieve?
- Can you operate under the constant threat of fear?

Yes, they are negative questions. And most experienced business people will say they are spot-on. I want to start with the final point because I think that fear is one of the most misunderstood and mishandled of all the personal traits that influence a business owner.

RECOGNISE YOUR FEAR

Every person who ever started or ran a business has felt fear. Rupert Murdoch, Kerry Packer, Gina Rinehart and Richard Branson have all felt fear. It's part of the territory. A new business means uncertainty, stepping into the unknown, making financial commitments and a chance of losing money and reputation. The same concerns weigh on the person who has had a business for fifteen years: major contracts fall over, prices drop, costs rise, the Aussie dollar ruins an export market, the oil price makes a business venture uneconomic, a government ruling stops a development. It is normal for humans to feel fear when faced with the chance of loss and, when the likelihood of those things draws closer, the fear levels can overwhelm the more optimistic parts of our personalities. As canvassed above, start by acknowledging fear—it's amazing how much power it loses once you chase it into the light; always position fear next to all the positives that are happening around it; and have a strategy for dealing with it (mine is exercise, positive thoughts and yoga).

WORKING TOO HARD

There are hundreds of papers and research results you can find on the internet about the negative effects on people who work too hard: mental problems, heart problems, blood pressure problems, ulcers, family breakdown and a constant state of exhaustion. It's all true. I have spent most of my business-owning life rising at 5.30 in the morning and going until midnight. When something needs to be fixed in a business of mine, I go hard until I fix it.

And it has a negative effect after a while. I can not moralise about this because when the work has to be done, I work the hours. However, I also watch my diet (I order a green salad with every meal), I exercise daily—walking, running, boxing, yoga—and I find time several times a week to have some reflective time, sitting on a park bench in the Botanic Gardens or swimming in the ocean.

STRESS

Stress is slightly different to just overworking or simply being scared. It doesn't freeze you or lure you into bad decisions, like fear does. And it doesn't exhaust you the way that overwork can. Stress usually mounts when there are too many decisions to make and the information isn't completely clear and there seems to be deadlines on everything, or else the worst is going to happen. This can happen several times a month in some businesses, usually because the owner has taken on too much or the right staff haven't been employed or there are too many things to do. This kind of frantic juggling is very common among private business owners, and it is not healthy for the owner or for the business. My own lesson in stress—learned the hard way—is that it is almost always a function of time. When I think back on some of the states I could get myself into as a younger man, the thing that was common to all of those situations was that I'd run myself out of time and I'd go out of my mind trying to do a week's work in a day. The trick, therefore, to taming stress, is to take control of time. You can take control of your time by doing two things: hire good people to take responsibilities and share the load; and be more intense about the business on a constant basis, thus eliminating the last-minute panic cycle that so many businesses exist in. Try introducing a daily urgency (not stress) into your business and you find time coming under control. Try this motto: if it's worth doing, it's worth doing now!

LOSING YOUR PASSION

It's sad when you see a business owner who used to be bright-eyed about the enterprise and its prospects reduced to a sense of going through the motions. Generally speaking, when I deal with this kind of business owner or high-level employee, I'm seeing someone who let the fire go out and forgot what their purpose and passions were. In the front of this book I suggested that among the personal tools that a business owner had to bring to the job was purpose. When you see someone who's forgotten why they're doing what they're doing, you see why purpose is not just some new-age hogwash but is actually a part of your business tool kit. Knowing why you're putting yourself through so much hassle is part of staying focused. When I find things getting on top of me, I try to skew my schedule back to the exercise, the yoga and the reflective time that I mentioned earlier. Another way of rediscovering your purpose and your passion is to do something for someone else. Helping out at a charity, volunteering at a PCYC, mowing the lawn for an elderly neighbour. Sometimes when we've lost the flame, what we have to do is give to someone who needs. It's very different to selling to someone who wants.

BURDENS OF LEADERSHIP

Unfortunately for every business owner, the role of leadership is never over. The clock never stops, you never take a true holiday you can delegate but you can't outsource leadership. There are other ways to deal with this, and I'll list a few below. But this is the raw, honest nature of the problem: the owner never stops being the owner, and while it's the managerial roles that gnaw at them with stress and fear, it's the role of leader that sits on their shoulders as a permanent weight. If this starts to feel like a burden rather than a challenge, they will shirk these responsibilities and the business will lose its way.

GETTING YOURSELF OUT OF THE WAY

Okay, so there are negative aspects to owning a business. Now I want to give you a few ideas about how to deal with some of the personal toll.

There is a word used by people outside of business which is actually a compliment to those of us inside it: ruthless. To be ruthless is to act without conscience or without fear of losing reputation or standing. Ruthless business people can sack half their workforce without even thinking about it, if it means maintaining a decent profit margin. Or so the media tells us.

First up, I'll admit that many people who've worked for me or written about me in the past have used the word 'ruthless', and not as a compliment. I don't always take this personally because sometimes—from their perspective—they've been right. But I would point out that there are two very different meanings of ruthless, as seen from the business owner's viewpoint. The first type of ruthless person is someone who is mean, selfish and often acting negatively out of ego-gratification. It's a power-trip. But the other kind of ruthless is the kind that I fall into, and that's the detached business owner who tries to make decisions for the welfare of the entire enterprise. Sometimes they are unpopular decisions but they are made for the greater good.

It is this second type of ruthlessness that good business owners should think about cultivating and practise on a daily basis. And this type of ruthlessness begins with getting your own ego and pride and anger out of the way. I believe—having dealt with medical people and spoken with hundreds of business people who suffer stress and unhappiness in business—that an essential way of protecting your personal self is to get your personal self out of the way.

What do I mean? Well, I think that when fear, stress and exhaustion overwhelm business owners, it is an accident of outlook rather than a medical inevitability. It happens because the owner's ego has joined with the business; they've merged at an emotional or psychological level with the operations and results of their business. This happens to senior employees, too, by the way.

But how do they get so attached? There might be something about this business that the owner feels personally responsible for or drawn to, and it's this aspect that an owner will favour in the misguided belief that their kindness or affection is good for the business. It rarely is.

By allowing your own identity to blend with that of the business, you invite problems that can become harder to undo the longer they go on. For instance, you may favour an employee because they started the business with you or because they belong to your family. You might continue to use a troublesome supplier because of old loyalties, or you still use an inadequate IT system because someone's son is doing the work for half price. Sometimes it's as simple as refusing to replace the printer that doesn't work.

I recommend a certain detachment from the business. By creating detachment you can train yourself to see the business as a thing in itself, and therefore something that needs to be tweaked and tuned to maintain its financial health.

The person who has no detachment from the business entity is often stuck in a rut. They don't fall into this situation because they're 'weak'—it happens because they're so immersed in the daily workings of the business that the enterprise becomes an extension of the self. Once the owner has done this, they've put themselves on the same level as everyone and everything—they've become part of the furniture, too close to see the flaws, too immersed to be strategic, too enmeshed in the daily problems to be a leader, and directed by fear and defined by stress.

When you get in the way of your own business, the results can be seen in your inability to strategise and, sometimes, your eroding mental health. Strategy is almost impossible to contemplate or execute if you haven't detached yourself from the emotional gravity of the business. Strategy, by its very nature, requires you to be able to see the business and its parts from a removed perspective, so you can clearly see where it should go and how it could get there. When you think of strategy, think of generals looking down at armies on a war table: you can't think strategically if you're in the trenches.

The same applies to maintaining your mental health. When you own a business, it's very easy to slip into a lifestyle of total immersion. In this state, you work closely with employees, contractors and clients and your identity blends into the business. Pretty soon, all of the business concerns—from signing a major new supply contract to the reordering of fax paper—become your responsibility. And because you're blended with the business, your employees turn immediately to you for *every* decision. You can drown in this, and it is all of your own making. It burns people out and brings on depression and all sorts of associated stress disorders such as alcohol abuse and panic attacks.

I'm as prone to falling into a business as anyone. I'm hardworking, I'm intense and I aim high. However, I've always had good support systems and people willing to give me an early warning. Here are some ideas about how to create some detachment—or emotional distance—from your business.

DELEGATE

One of the best ways to create some distance between yourself and the business is to delegate tasks to employees. Even if you only have two employees, you have to start by creating responsibilities for *them* so you can manage their performance rather than becoming part of the daily grind. In industries such as hospitality, where the owner works alongside employees, you must delegate even small jobs to clear the decks for you to think about management, strategy, finance, and so on.

USE YOUR EXPERTS

If there are tasks that cannot be delegated to employees, then talk to your outsourced professionals about functions they can take up to ease your load. Aspects such as payroll and dealing with banks can be handed to your accountants. Use an IT contractor to deal with all the computers, upgrades and maintenance.

LISTEN TO YOUR ADVISERS

Everyone in business needs someone to act as a reality check. Good advisers—usually accountants or management consultants—relish this role and also understand your need to detach from the intensity of the daily action. Often it's the adviser who drops by once a month who sees the things you can't see: the dirty carpet, the lazy employee, the spelling mistake on your new brochure.

MENTORS

You can't look these people up in the Yellow Pages and many people will run a business for decades without ever having a mentor. But if you're lucky enough to have a mentor, use them to help you take a helicopter position on your business, even if it's just for a couple of hours each week. Good mentors don't want to get their hands dirty in your business—they want to talk about issues and ideas, hints and lessons. These are the kinds of conversations that help provide you with some critical distance.

PARTNERS

When you have a partner in a business, the skills and capital you each bring is only part of the strength. When there's more than one of you, there is no excuse to fall into the traps I have described. Partners are a mutual support mechanism as much as anything else and they have to help one another have some distance. One warning about partners: it is disastrous if one is left to do all the nuts-and-bolts while the other gets to be strategic and distant. Partners means *partners*.

CREATE SYSTEMS

It's one thing to delegate, but have you got the systems to deal with it? A system could be a regular Monday morning meeting where you assign work and responsibility for the week and check on the progress of the things you delegated. A system could be rewriting the staff work chart so that more of the minor decisions are handed down the line and you can refocus on big decisions and business development. Create a system and you further detach yourself because you don't have to explain yourself every time you want someone to take the responsibility.

•

If the first job is to physically remove yourself from so much of the minutiae of the business, the second job is to use a few psychological tricks to distance yourself from the maelstrom. Ultimately, you want the strength to be in the business but not drowning under it.

CHAPTER 20

STEPPING AWAY
FROM YOURSELF

Every person who hopes to make a fist of business ownership has to start, in my opinion, by knowing themselves. But the corollary to knowing what drives you is being able to step away from yourself.

The Oracle at Delphi may say 'Man Know Thyself', and this is the beginning point for all things. But the next phase is being able to look at yourself from the outside.

What does this mean? It means that whether you're running a business or trying to get ahead in someone else's business, you have to develop in yourself the ability to disassociate from the minute-to-minute fight and see yourself as an actor in the scenario. Great sportspeople, actors and performers are able to do this. It means distinguishing yourself from the objective reality you operate in. It doesn't mean you can only see the scenario from a distance, but it also doesn't mean that you can only experience a situation through your own senses. You must develop the ability to do both.

To give you an analogy: the scientist wants to understand motivation and behaviour, so she sets up a maze, with a water dispenser down one end and a red light at the other. Then she puts a mouse in the maze and watches.

You are the mouse.

You must also be the scientist.

You are the subject (the mouse) and you are also the object (the experiment).

Before I explain myself, let me make this observation: Every successful person I have ever known uses the above technique to ensure they are always seeing things accurately. As a philosopher might say, seeing the thing itself for what it is. This technique of dissociation is crucial for busy, ambitious people, for a number of reasons. The biggest is that it helps you develop the critical side of yourself rather than just the side that participates. If all you're doing in a business is participating, then you're not letting your higher faculties operate and it's these faculties that the business owner needs in order to be strategic and be a leader.

I worked out almost twenty years ago that as far as personalities go, I am far more the observer (the scientist) than I am the participator (the mouse). I enjoy standing back and assessing what is happening and working it out. I enjoy observing and explaining the objective rather than having to always participate subjectively. So I have had to work on social skills and social involvement in order to balance my more aloof instincts. I don't mind this process and in fact I believe it has given me a better approach to business because I understand that there are two ways to experience the world and I am practised at both. It has given me a capacity to separate myself by understanding perspectives, and I believe most people can use this themselves.

Perhaps the worst side effect of being unable to separate your objective self from the subjective self is that you tend to collapse thoughts and emotion into your actual business identity. People who cannot separate these sides of themselves end up 'being the thought'. This means that they find it hard to acknowledge something negative in the business without also feeling personally bad. They can't observe something for what it is—they have to turn it into a feeling . . . that they feel. When you think of how many problems and setbacks that we have to deal with every week in a business, this identification between the thought and the person is too overwhelming. Especially since the owner is the leader and is supposed to be offering wise counsel and critical distance when there are setbacks. The owner is not supposed to be going into a funk because sales dipped.

We have to keep ourselves separated from the event and the emotion, because as business owners it's our job to stay focused on goals and on the possibilities of the market we operate in. I see the market like the universe: a field of infinite possibilities. Anything can happen and I have to keep myself prepared and open, ready for anything. But if I can't observe the infinite—if all I can *feel* is what just went wrong—then I am losing my perspective and my ability to operate in and with the market. Instead I become a slave to a single disappointment in my business while there's an infinity of possible events happening all around me.

STANDING ASIDE

The ability to stand aside from yourself can resolve a good number of the stress-related problems that lead to exhaustion, burnout and drug abuse problems. But the reason everyone in business should practise detachment is that it allows for clear, open thinking in an environment where a lot of noise is produced.

Along with learning how to disassociate yourself, also learn to gravitate towards people who are more open-minded, creative and constructive. In a business environment, where there are orders to fill, consignments to ship and money to chase, we can find ourselves firmly shoved in the 'box'. Try to balance up your time so you are talking with as many creative people as you are technical types. Creative and constructive people can stand outside themselves and have an idea non-judgementally—a design is just a design; a drawing is a thing unto itself. But many technical people can't do this: they censor themselves before they even have the thought.

Start by standing aside from your subjective thinking-acting self, and observing yourself in the objective scenario. There are a number of reasons to look into this.

MAKING MORE TIME

Firstly, standing aside gives you a sense of time. As covered earlier, one of the problems that driven people run into is that there never seems to be enough time. So they start waking earlier, working longer, going to bed later and sleeping less. And in their working hours they try to get more done by using scheduling software, using email on their iPhones, using laptops as they wait at the departure lounge or in the back of a cab. It creates what we call the 'crush': a sensation that multiple deadlines are closing in, all of them more drastic than the last, with more at stake and more to lose and less room for error.

When people are feeling crushed, it spills into all areas of their lives and they have to reclaim time. Everyone who is getting crushed should think about this: what if I could stand outside my body and my mind, and see this situation as a scenario in which I am one of the actors? The answer is, once you become good at it, you have more time because you make better decisions . . .

JUDGEMENT

In the two sports I love—rugby league and boxing—there are contestants who stand above the other great contestants because they have 'vision'. In rugby league, this is said of the great five-eighths Wally Lewis, Andrew Johns and Darren Lockyer. They are playing the same game as their team-mates and opponents and they are in the same timeframe: 80 minutes. Yet they seem to have more time to do what they have to do. They seem unhurried and also able to make good judgements about where to kick, who to pass to, where to place the defensive line. They are seeing themselves as if from afar, while also being in the moment themselves. It gives them the time and vision to make better decisions than other players. Business owners can do this too: by standing outside the immediate, subjective moment, you can take away the panic and concentrate on what opportunities exist.

ENDURANCE

I know from personal experience that when I'm being successful with this policy of disassociation, I can give myself more energy and concentration as I go through the day. I can keep my mind sharper for longer and I can stay snappy in a meeting or negotiation as others are yawning and fidgeting. Being able to stand outside myself seems to extend my batteries.

CLEAR VIEWPOINT

Being able to unhitch yourself from your own subjective wants and fears allows you to make much clearer assessments of what is going on around you because the way you act and react can be appropriate for the entire scenario rather than what you need. Sometimes in a group meeting, a problem might come up and before you know it, the participants are speaking from the position of their own fears and desires. They aren't talking about the organisation or the margin versus volume debate: they're talking about how they look in front of their peers, what the problem is going to do to their bonus and how badly they want a promotion. It's all subjective, it ignores what actually is happening and it's contagious. One person descending into this perspective can bring the whole room with them—it's a stress cauldron. As a leader, you can't stop people being like this, but you can stop yourself doing it and you can bring the discussion back to what's real.

KEEP QUESTIONING

One way of trying to stand aside and give yourself more time and room to move in your mind is to remain at a slightly paranoid state. I don't mean having delusions and needing medication; I mean, become a constant asker of questions rather than the person who is permanently called on to provide answers.

One of the constant factors among business owners who are stressed and burning out is that they have become the 'go-to' person and it is wearing them down. When I slip into the paranoia phase, I turn this around and make myself the questioner rather than the answerer. Make this a habit: to question your staff and partners rather than constantly being the sounding board. There's always something to fix in a business and by forcing the conversations around so that you ask most of the questions, not only are you finetuning the business but you're relieving your stress by making others do the thinking.

THE POWER OF DEDUCTIVE REASONING

The problem of 'being your thought' or of being too subjective about your business is not confined to business owners. The entire society we live in is driven by a subjective force that verges on mass narcissism. We are sold products, urged how to vote and even conduct relationships based on what we are supposed to feel about ourselves. This is not a very good environment for a business owner because the ability to succeed entails as much objective reality as it does subjective feeling.

The trick to keeping an objective eye on the world is a system of thinking called 'deductive reasoning'. We recognise it by the basic argument that goes like this:

All Australians are human
All humans are mortal
Therefore, all Australians are mortal

It is simple, and it has helped me through many complex ideas when I've needed to think about what is actual rather than what has been projected to me.

One of the drawbacks of subjective thinking is that it both tricks you and enslaves you. And this is very dangerous if you're trying to deal with something as dynamic as a market. Firstly, if the only way you can deal with issues is by projecting your own feelings about yourself onto others, then you will trick yourself into thinking that your subjective feelings are the same thing as objective reality. They are not. This can have catastrophic results in how you market your goods and what you believe the market wants. You can get it totally wrong and it's your own subjective mind that tricked you.

This also enslaves you. A constant feedback loop of assuming that what you want is what everyone wants can trap you into bad decisions and poor reactions to bad sales. Subjective people say things like, 'The audience was wrong', or 'The buyers didn't understand what they were doing', or 'The voters got it wrong'. This is very, very bad business thinking, if this is all you have.

A business person has to have the capacity to stand back from the fray, to dissociate from their own efforts and their own subjective desire to sell products. Most business transactions are actually fairly logical—just remind yourself of why you buy goods and services. Kerry Packer used to say that a good advertising campaign was simple: 'Tell them what it is, how much it costs and where they can get it.'

If you're trapped in seeing the world through your eyes and your eyes only, then you are missing the chance to see all of the possibilities by explaining things objectively. Deductive reasoning is one of the ways you can break this cycle, which, as I say, is all around us, especially in journalism, politics and advertising. We are used to consuming a diet of someone's viewpoint, so we think this is a normal way of seeing the world. It's not. If you want to engage with something as infinite and dynamic as a marketplace, then you'll have to practise seeing the objective reality of what it actually is.

Start with deductive reasoning and the syllogism. It'll help you see things more clearly and also help divorce your essential self from your business. Don't be the thought.

CHAPTER 21

LOOKING AFTER YOURSELF

Here's my final word of advice: spare a thought for yourself.

People who are drawn to business can get so engrossed in the daily cut and thrust of the thing that they forget to put something aside for themselves, forget to look after their health and their families, and forget to have a laugh. Don't be like so many business owners and simply hope that if you own a small business for twenty years, you'll sell it one day and walk off with a big bag of money, and then you'll suddenly be happy and healthy.

Through this book you've seen what it takes to drive a business price from a valuation and from many KPIs that build to a price. It's a strategy and a slog to create a capital gain from a business in relatively fast time. But it will be no easier simply because you hold onto it for two decades. And just having the money at the end of the journey won't give you happiness and health. You need something to retire on, and here are some ideas.

FINANCIAL PLANNING

Business owners traditionally have three ways of providing something for the future. They sell, they leverage equity, or they make retirement investments through their self-managed superannuation fund:

- **Sell**—The business owner can sell for an earnings multiple, as a trade sale or an acquisition. Regardless of the size of the business, an owner really needs to have a decent lead-time to make the sale (at least a year) and also needs to bring on advisers. The difference in the sale price—due to something small like a rebranding or a costs restructure—can be as much as $100 000 in a small business, more in a medium-sized enterprise. This is your retirement savings—make sure you get what you can.
- **Equity**—Equity is the difference between assets and liabilities and gives the owner the opportunity to diversify their business interests. If you build a business so you have several million in equity in the enterprise, this could well be your retirement nest egg, yet it's all riding in one entity. Having strong equity gives you the opportunity to sell off parts of it and put the capital into other investments, such as property, shares and agriculture. Having said this, many business people prefer to keep their equity invested where they understand it and can control it. I understand this attitude. But you still have to provide for you.
- **Retirement savings**—There are many benefits that business owners enjoy from selling their business and transferring the capital into a superannuation fund. These funds can be

self-managed or managed by a large retail outfit. The important thing is that there are many tax laws and conditions that apply to the generous tax concessions for contributing sale proceeds to your own superannuation. You need advice on this, not only for what you can and can't do, but for timing as well. The government recognises that many business people build up their retirement nest eggs in their business, and they are generous about investing this money. But you must do it according to the rules.

I understand fully the reluctance that many long-time business people have to investing their money with fund managers into the stock market. It is hard to lose control of management decisions once you have done it yourself for so long. However, allowing professional mangers to do this is not so unlike using advisers in your business. When you need the added value, reach for an expert.

Looking after your health

The business world takes so much time and effort and what usually happens is that the financial goals of the business owner take over from other equally important goals such as physical health, mental wellbeing and spiritual fulfilment. See my comments on separating yourself in the previous chapter.

BODY

You have to try and do something physical at least twice a week. You may think you don't have the time but you do have the time, you just choose to spend it on the business. Doctors say that good exercise is anything that lifts your heart rate enough so you pant and work up a light sweat. If you do this for a few times a week, you can stay reasonably fit. Activities you might consider include walking, golf, tennis and swimming. Being fit keeps you more relaxed and able to stay alert for longer in your working life. Being fit is an asset.

MIND

Not everything that goes into your mind can be spreadsheets and sales reports or you'll become a little mad. To keep a healthy mind, try to maintain friendships or associations with non-business people and read non-business material. For instance, read a general newspaper every morning and stay active at the golf club, footy club or the surf lifesaving club. Your mind, in order to stay in optimum health, needs a variety of stimulation. Get away from whiteboards and PowerPoint when you can. Go see a band, visit a vineyard, learn another language.

SPIRIT

Business people in particular, and Australians in general, hate to talk about spirit. I have touched on spirit when talking about the need for a purpose in a business, and the same goes for your life outside of business. You need a reason, you need something that touches your heart, you need to laugh out loud. Staying close to family and old friends is one way of ensuring you keep in touch with this. Or you might want to join a charity and get your staff involved, too. One of the hardest things in business is to work hard and have success and maintain your spirit. It's an important part of you and only you can keep it going.

PERSONAL DEVELOPMENT

In keeping with the concept of separating yourself so you can see things from a distance is the notion of knowing that you are still a person, not simply the 'boss'. I have seen enough retired business owners to know that the aimless and restless ones wish they'd kept a personal hobby going during all those hard years when they were building a business, employing people and supporting a family.

You need to have something that you enjoy and that has *nothing* to do with business—yachting, driving a sports car, going to the opera, skiing, learning to play drums, doing painting classes or yoga. There has to be a safety valve in your life where your brain can focus totally on the thing that you do for yourself, for your own reasons. The development of a business and staff is an exhausting exercise—you need to spend a few hours of the week on you.

SABBATICALS

Everyone needs a holiday. But people who work 70- or 80-hour weeks and carry all the responsibility for a business on their own shoulders need to take an extended leave once a decade. I understand how easy it is to say this, and how hard it is to do. And I also know that business owners will often put in place these HR schemes for their senior managers, but never take them themselves. I get it, believe me. But sabbaticals are common in the large corporations and big law and accounting firms for good reason: namely, for all the issues I've raised in this chapter. People who can literally get away from it all for an extended break return refreshed, with their confidence back and with some good ideas in their head. They come back with mental energy. If you can't stand the thought of a two-month break, why not see it as a business boosting exercise?

•

In the end, business owners should stand outside themselves and see what is needed. You need to stay fit, happy and mentally sharp. Personal health and development might be one of the best KPIs you ever develop.

•

Lastly, for those about to go into business, I wish you good luck. Luck plays its part in this life we choose, whether we admit to it or not. When I was building Wizard Home Loans, I needed a partner in the business with influence and power in the capital markets. I decided that I wanted a large European investment bank in my business and we negotiated their shareholding for nine months. It was nine months of to-ing and fro-ing, arguments, counter-arguments, lots of lawyers and lots of stalemates. I earned something of a reputation during this time for being the stubborn, tough little guy from Australia who was prepared to get into an arm wrestle with the big guy from Europe.

The truth was I could see a good fit for this bank in my

business, but I didn't want to be forced to take a low price for their shareholding just because they were big and I was small.

In the ninth month, at a point when I wasn't sure if we were still negotiating, I got a call from out of the blue and the bank wanted to do the deal and basically at the price I wanted.

I found out later that things had changed at head office in Europe and this massive bank wanted a partnership of the type I was offering. In the end, I got lucky. It's just that it took me nine months of grind for fortune to turn my way.

If you can understand this lesson, you're well on your way.